BUSINESS BEHAVIOUR

Other Philip Allan economics titles

KLAUS HEIDENSOHN *Middlesex Polytechnic*

NICK ROBINSON *University of Reading*

BUSINESS BEHAVIOUR

an economic approach

Philip Allan

First published 1974 by
PHILIP ALLAN PUBLISHERS LIMITED
RED LION COTTAGE
MARKET PLACE
DEDDINGTON
OXFORD OX5 4SE

0 86003 000 8 (hardback)
0 86003 100 4 (paperback)

Illustrations by Oxford Illustrators
Printed in Great Britain by Holywell Press, Oxford

Contents

Preface

There are so many texts on the theory of the firm that one must have good reasons for adding to their number. In our case, two important considerations made us write this text.

Firstly, although microeconomics and the theory of the firm form a vital aspect of the economics teaching on courses in economics and business studies, there is an apparent lack of books offering a suitably comprehensive and comprehensible treatment of business behaviour. The available texts either restrict their analysis to profit maximisation or, if they do extend their analysis by considering alternative objectives, the treatment becomes too advanced for many students. In this text, we discuss business behaviour under alternative objective functions but keep the analysis simple without sacrificing rigour.

Secondly, as students and teachers we have felt some dissatisfaction with the emphasis on equilibrium situations and the lack of predictions with empirical content in much of traditionally taught economics. Hence our preoccupation with the response of firms to changes in their situations and our stress on the way economics can help to predict and illustrate features of management actions.

We are indebted to a number of students and teachers with whom we exchanged views on this subject. We should like, in particular, to thank Professor Maurice Peston and Professor David Laidler for helpful comments on an earlier version. Nic Zafiris kindly read and commented upon parts of the manuscript in its incipient stages and contributed by writing a chapter on the dynamics of business behaviour. All remaining shortcomings of this book are, of course, our sole responsibility.

KH/NR

CHRISTINA: *This is a yukky book*

1
Economics and business behaviour

1.1 Introduction

Since the emergence of modern or Keynesian economics it has been customary to divide economics into two major fields: *macroeconomics* and *microeconomics*. At the risk of oversimplifying the issues we can say that macroeconomics is the study of broad aggregates in an economy and that it tries to answer the important question of what determines the level of economic activity, measured by concepts like national income or the level of employment. Microeconomics, on the other hand, is a study of the behaviour of the individual decision making units in an economy; it tries to provide answers to another important question: how to allocate scarce resources among competing interests.

Macroeconomic analysis is useful in that it enables us better to appreciate public policy measures related to issues such as employment, inflation, the balance of payments and growth. Macroeconomics is useful to the businessman who is interested in acquiring knowledge of the economic trends that exist in an economy, since these trends contribute to the performance of firms and cannot therefore be ignored.

What are the uses to which microeconomics can be put? In the first instance, microeconomics is a general inquiry into the working of (market) economies. At a more sophisticated level this philosophical inquiry has led to the development of 'welfare economics' which is concerned with a discussion of the criteria that make one economic system more efficient than another; welfare economics provides a framework for the development of policy measures designed to increase the efficiency of an economy. There is, however, another use to which microeconomic analysis can be put. Because the microeconomic system of analysis of resource allocation in an economy is based on a study of the behaviour of small units, it can be used to study the behaviour of particular agents in the economy. In conducting an analysis of the behaviour of economic agents we can focus attention on consumers or producers; we may even be interested in studying the behaviour of particular markets.

One special field within the analysis of the behaviour of economic agents is generally known as the *theory of the firm*. The meaning of this term is, however, not unequivocal. In fact, a survey of the literature reveals that 'theory of the firm' has been used in four different ways. First of all, it can mean an analysis of how objectives are determined in a business organisation. Because great stress is laid in this kind of analysis on the organisational aspects of business and the hierarchical relationships that exist within business, this approach is also known as the *organisational* or *behavioural approach* to the theory of the firm. Secondly, one may refer to the development of techniques that are used by business in an attempt to achieve particular objectives. Examples of such techniques are decision theory, operational research, and programming. Thirdly, 'theory of the firm' may describe the analysis of the reaction of firms to changes in their environment. Finally, it can also be understood to mean a combination of the approaches to firms' behaviour just described.

In what follows we shall adopt an economic approach to the study of the firm. This approach will take the form of developing predictions with empirical content in the sense that they enable us to understand observable features of firms' decisions. In attempting to analyse business behaviour one has to be aware that firms experience changes in their market situations, in their cost conditions, in the level of taxation they face, and so on. How do firms respond to such changes? It is this response that we shall seek to explain. But before we embark on our analysis, it is important to clarify the methodology we shall be using.

1.2 Method of approach

The methodology we shall adopt is the traditional one of model construction. Models consist of a set of assumptions and a set of conclusions that have been deduced logically from those assumptions. In constructing an economic model we have to make assumptions about the technical aspects of the problem we want to investigate and assumptions about the behaviour of people (their aims and rationality). Needless to say, in making the assumptions, it is not possible to make them in such a way that they are complete and exact reflections of the real world; we are forced to abstract. In abstracting we must, of course, try to select and include in our model those aspects of the real world that are important and we must make relevant assumptions about them. Also, in abstracting we may find that many apparently different situations are similar.

How do we find out whether the model we have constructed with a particular set of assumptions and yielding a set of conclusions is useful? One may be tempted to suggest that one test of the model would be whether it contains realistic assumptions. But to criticise the validity of the assumptions of a model, although easy enough, is a futile undertaking: it is in the very nature of a model that it requires abstraction and simplification! Clearly, a more interesting question to ask is whether with the aid of a model we can predict correctly how a firm will react, in terms of the choice of its strategic variables such as price, output, advertising, staff expenditure, etc., when experiencing a change in, for example, profits taxation. Suppose that a model A, based on the assumption that firms pursue profit maximisation, predicts that firms will not be affected by higher taxes on profits, i.e. will change neither price nor output nor expenditure on advertising. Suppose further that we have another model B based on the assumption of non-profit maximising behaviour and that according to this model firms would change their prices, output levels and advertising expenditure in response to higher profit taxation. Then, if we observe in the real world behaviour that is consistent with the prediction produced by model A, we would accept our model A as useful. If, on the other hand, observed behaviour appears to be consistent with the conclusions emerging from model B, we would give preference to model B over model A.

The method adopted by economists (sometimes referred to as 'positive economics') can best be illustrated by looking at the theoretical foundations of the aspects of business behaviour that will be considered in this book.

In operating a business one is confronted with some basic conditions which determine the possibilities of producing and selling a particular product: revenues are an expression of the sales firms are likely to achieve at particular prices and advertising levels; costs give some indication of the outlay necessary to procure the factors of production involved; the market structure defines the degree of competition with which the firm is faced. But although the assumptions we make about the revenue and cost aspects, and the market structure, provide us with the framework within which to construct our theory of firms' behaviour, they merely represent possible choices open to firms in their operation.

To complete the construction of our economic theory of business behaviour we have to add one further element—we have to make an assumption about the goals governing business behaviour. *Maximising* (or *optimising*) and *satisficing* behaviour present themselves as alternatives in this context. If we assume maximising behaviour, we imply that the firms' objective is to maximise some particular function—profits, sales, output, etc. Satisficing behaviour, on the other hand, means that firms are not interested in maximising anything, but merely set themselves certain 'aspiration levels'—a certain return on the capital employed, a certain market share, a certain sales level, a certain profit level. Throughout our analysis we shall be assuming that firms' behaviour conforms to the hypothesis of 'maximising' behaviour. In making this assumption we do not propose to ignore the valuable contributions the 'organisational' school has made by focussing attention on the processes by which firms reach their decisions. The purpose of our analysis, however, is different as we pointed out earlier; we want to study the outcome of firms' decisions and this we can achieve only if we derive predictions from our models. Predictions about behaviour can, however, only be derived if we assume that firms are maximising or minimising something.

The basic conditions under which firms operate being defined and specified and an assumption about the firms' objectives being made, we are in a position to draw conclusions about the choices firms make. The conclusions following from the set of assumptions in our models are derived via a process of logical deduction, which can take the form of verbal reasoning, can make use of (usually) two-dimensional diagrams, or can rely on mathematics. Sometimes the implications of a set of assumptions are seen through the use of computer-simulation models.

The next step in our approach is to find out whether the conclusions (or predictions) from our model are consistent with observed behaviour. If our predicted behaviour of the firm under certain circumstances is consistent with observed behaviour then we would say that our model is acceptable and can continue to be used. It is of course possible that two models based on different sets of assumptions produce the same result in terms of predicting a particular behavioural pattern. In such an event, one could not use observed behaviour that was consistent with the predicted behaviour as evidence supporting both models. It would be necessary under these circumstances to find predictions that were unique to either of these two models. A simple example will help to illustrate the problem posed by discriminatory testing. Suppose we assume that a firm is interested in maximising profits and that our model of the firm's behaviour predicts that the firm would respond to an increase in demand by raising the price of its product. If by making an alternative assumption about the firm's goal we could derive the same prediction, there is no way of telling which of the two behavioural assumptions leads to the 'better' predictions. If in testing a model we establish that the observed behaviour is at variance with the predicted behaviour, we would have to reject the model or possibly revise it. In revising a model we may have to modify the assumptions we have made and possibly add to their number. Figure 1.1 illustrates the methodological approach we have adopted in our analysis of firms' behaviour.

Two final comments about economic methodology are necessary. First, the way we make predictions about a firm's behaviour or response is by assuming that the firm at the outset of our analysis is in 'equilibrium'. We start with a purely *static* analysis. We then assume that the firm is experiencing a change in its circumstances which may or may not persuade it to take particular courses of action like changing its price, output, advertising expenditure and the like. If we postulate that the firm as a result of its response reaches a new state of equilibrium after some time, we can then compare one state of equilibrium with another. This is known as *comparative static* analysis. Second, the

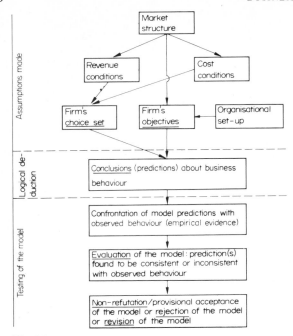

Fig:1.1

reader is warned that for the validation of our models of business behaviour it is not necessary that businessmen actually and literally use the models we develop when reaching their decisions. The economic agents whose behaviour we want to explain may behave in the way our models predict without consciously using any model. Clearly, such models would still be useful.[1]

1.3 Programme of analysis

In pursuing our aim of analysing firms' behaviour (using the method briefly outlined in the previous section) we shall adopt the following programme. We shall first (in Chapter 2) discuss some of the basic conditions which determine the revenue and cost aspects

[1]For a discussion of this point see, for example, M. Friedman, The methodology of positive economics, *Essays in Positive Economics,* University of Chicago Press 1953.

of running a business. Our next step (Chapter 3) will be to consider one objective of firms' behaviour, profit maximisation, and to derive conclusions about the choices profit maximising firms make and how they change them if confronted with certain changes in their operating conditions (changes in revenue, cost, taxation). Chapter 4 represents an extension of the profit maximising model and deals with more complicated and realistic situations (price discrimination, advertising, multiplant and multiproduct firms).

Chapters 5 and 6 continue the analysis of the choices firms can be expected to make and how they may respond to changes in revenue, costs and taxation; but now the assumption of profit maximising behaviour is dropped. In Chapter 5 we assume throughout that firms are interested in, and actively pursue, output maximisation. In Chapter 6 we assume that maximum sales revenue is their goal.

In Chapter 7 we deal with the last of the four models of the theory of the firm presented in this book. Rather than assuming that a single objective like maximum profit, output or sales is the firm's aim, we base our analysis on the notion that firms' managers pursue the aim of maximising the satisfaction derived from different aspects of running a business (profit, staff expenditure, 'perks'). Again, as in the treatment of the simple profit maximising, output maximising and sales revenue maximising models, we focus attention on the choices the managerial-satisfaction maximising firm makes and how these choices are likely to be affected by changes in revenue, costs and taxation. In Chapter 8 we show how the simple comparative static approach may be extended to deal with the dynamic aspects of firms' decision making over time. In the final chapter we summarise, compare and evaluate the various predictions emerging from our models of the theory of the firm. This necessitates a discussion of the problems involved in testing the hypotheses under consideration and an attempt to judge the predictive content of the models presented in terms of the empirical evidence available.

Suggestions for further reading

Microeconomics

D. Laidler, *Introduction to Microeconomics*, Philip Allan 1974.
F.M. Scherer, *Industrial Market Structure and Economic Performance*, University of Chicago Press 1970.

Economic methodology

C.D. Harbury, *An Introduction to Economic Behaviour*, Fontana 1972. (See Chapter 9 especially.)
M. Friedman, *Essays in Positive Economics*, University of Chicago Press 1953. (See Part I especially.)
R.G. Lipsey, *An Introduction to Positive Economics*, (3rd edn) Weidenfeld and Nicolson 1971. (See Chapter 1 especially.)
R.M. Cyert and J.G. March, *Theory of the Firm*, Prentice Hall 1963. (Appendix A)

Introduction to the theory of the firm

J.K. Galbraith, *The New Industrial State*, Penguin 1969.
J.R. Cable, Business objectives and the theory of firm, *Economics*, Spring 1967.
B.J. Loasby, Management objectives and the theory of the firm, *Journal of Industrial Economics*, July 1967.

2
Costs and revenues

2.1 Introduction

In this chapter we shall discuss the theoretical foundations upon which economists base their analyses of firms' behaviour. In this area of study, as in many others, economists follow the methodology outlined at the start of Chapter 1, by first abstracting from many of the complications of the real world so that they can consider a particularly simple model and then introducing complications to see to what extent the conclusions reached from a consideration of the simple model have to be modified. We shall do the same here, discussing the simple model in Chapters 2 and 3 and examining some of the complications in Chapter 4.

Our simple model will be a firm which produces only one product, which sells each unit of the product at the same price and which produces all of its output in a single plant. Even within a firm with so simple a structure a number of decisions have to be taken about the price to be charged for the product, the number of units to be produced, the number of jobs to be offered and so on. In order to arrive at their decisions the firm's decision makers must weigh up the effects of a very large number of factors, some of which are within their own control and some of which are not. To make the process more manageable these factors are often split into two groups according to whether they affect revenue or costs. Often one department, such as the sales department, is given the responsibility for examining those factors affecting revenue while another, such as the production department, is given the responsibility for examining those factors affecting costs. Of course, the results of each department's investigations have to be brought together at some time before final decisions can be taken but many firms find such a separation an efficient way of arriving at their important decisions. We shall make a similar separation when looking at the firm from our theoretical viewpoint.

2.2 Revenue

The examination of the firm's revenue position usually begins with a look at the determinants of the number of units which it can sell in any given period.

A firm's sales department may well devote considerable effort to finding out why people buy its products and the extent to which the number of units which can be sold changes in response to competitors' actions, the price charged and so on. It may sometimes be the case that it is impossible to identify any reasons why people buy its products or to find any systematic response to changes in factors such as price. However, these cases are rare and usually some important factors may be identified. These factors differ from firm to firm and from product to product. To illustrate our approach we shall select the factors which figure most frequently but we hope that by the time he has read Chapter 4 the reader who has a particular case in mind will be able to make his own list of factors by replacing some (or all) of ours by those which his experience suggests are important and will see how our methodology can be applied to the new list.

We shall assume that the firm's sales department identifies the following factors as important:

(i)   their product's price;
(ii)   the prices of similar products produced by other firms;
(iii) the average level of customers' incomes;
(iv)   government credit controls.

We shall further assume that the quantity which the firm can sell is greater:

(i)   the lower their product's price;
(ii)   the higher the prices of similar products produced by other firms;
(iii) the greater the average level of customers' incomes;
(iv)   the less severe government credit controls.

The factors listed above fall into two types. The last three are usually outside the firm's control and will determine the situation in which it must operate, while the first is within its control and forms part of the list of factors to be chosen by the firm's decision makers. To help in the making of such a choice the firm's sales department might well provide information about the likely effect of price on the quantity which can be sold. In the case of a well-established product the sales department could probably use its knowledge of the effects of past price changes to predict the effects of any changes which the firm's management may wish to consider. In the case of new products the sales department's problem is more difficult, but some evidence may be gained from test marketing in a particular region, from interviews in which potential customers are shown the product and asked to estimate its selling price and the number which they would buy at that price, from the issue of catalogues which quote different prices for different regions so that the sales department can compare the orders received from each region, and so on. More details of the way in which information about the effects of price changes can be obtained are given in the list of suggestions for further reading at the end of this chapter.

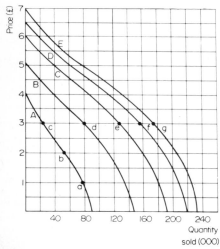

Fig:2.1

Such information may of course be presented in a number of ways ranging from detailed statistical tables to a verbal report by the firm's sales director.

Very often a graph such as Fig. 2.1 is found to be a convenient way of summarising information. Each curve in Fig. 2.1 shows the effect of price on the quantity which can be sold in one particular situation. Hence, if other firms decide upon certain prices, if the average level of customers' incomes is a certain amount per year and if the government decides upon a certain set of controls, then we use the curve labelled A to find that 75,000 units can be sold at a price of £1 per unit (point a), 50,000 units can be sold at a price of £2 per unit (point b), 24,000 units can be sold at a price of £3 per unit (point c) and so on. If the firm's situation changes then we use another curve. For example, if the average level of customers' incomes rises then we use the curve labelled B which indicates that a greater quantity can be sold at each price. If the average level of customers' income rises further we use the curve labelled C and so on.[1] Just as rises in customers' incomes shift the curve showing the relationship between quantity sold and price, so will changes in other firms' prices and in the severity of government credit controls. Hence each curve in Fig. 2.1 shows the relationship between price and quantity *while all other factors remain unchanged at particular values.* Should one of the other factors change then the relationship between price and quantity will be shown by a different curve. Curves such as these are known as *demand curves,* or more strictly as *own price demand curves.*

From the information given above the firm can calculate the sales revenue it will obtain from the various combinations of price and output which are open to it. Consider first the case of the firm in the situation giving rise to demand curve A. The firm can set a price of £3 per unit and sell 24,000 units thus producing a revenue of £72,000, or it can set a price of £2 per unit and sell 50,000 units thus producing a revenue of £100,000, or it can set a price of £1 per

[1]Successive curves need not exhibit the pattern shown here. Successive curves will be higher if people buy more of the product as their incomes increase (e.g. if the product is a car rather than a bicycle) and the successive spaces between them will decline if equal increases in income have declining effects on demand (i.e. if there is some sort of saturation level which puts an upper limit on the number of products which people wish to buy). The reader should sketch the curves which would correspond to different circumstances.

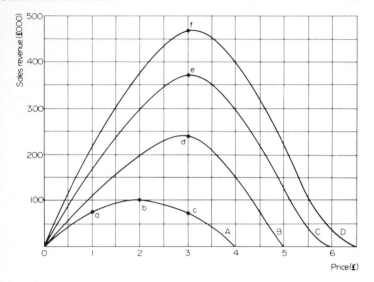

Fig:2.2

unit and sell 75,000 units thus producing a revenue of £75,000, and so on. Calculations such as these allow the firm to draw curve A in Fig. 2.2. (The labelled points in Fig. 2.2 correspond to those shown in Fig. 2.1.) Similarly, a situation giving rise to demand curve B will give rise to *sales revenue curve* B in Fig. 2.2, and so on.

Whether or not sales revenue rises or falls as the selling price is reduced and the quantity sold increased depends on the responsiveness of quantity sold to price. If the firm reduces its price then it now sells at the lower price all the units which it previously sold at the higher price and hence it forgoes revenue on the sale of these units. On the other hand, if the reduction in price allows the firm to sell more then it gains extra revenue from these new sales. If the gain from the new sales more than offsets the revenue forgone on the old sales then sales revenue will rise, but if it does not then sales revenue will fall. Clearly, the greater the increase in quantity sold the more likely it is that sales revenue will rise.

In terms of our example a decrease in price from £3 to £2 increases sales from 24,000 units to 50,000 units and hence increases sales revenue from £72,000 to £100,000. The increase of

£28,000 in sales revenue is made up of £24,000 forgone by selling the old units for £1 less together with £52,000 gained by selling an extra 26,000 units for £2 each. If the price is cut further to £1, sales increase from 50,000 units to 75,000 units but sales revenue falls from £100,000 to £75,000. The fall of £25,000 is made up of £50,000 forgone by selling the old units for £1 less together with £25,000 gained by selling an extra 25,000 units for £1 each.

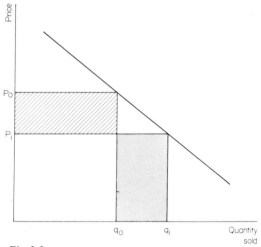

Fig:2.3

This is illustrated in Fig. 2.3 which shows a fall in price from P_0 to P_1 which produces an increase in quantity sold from q_0 to q_1. The shaded area, which is equal to the quantity sold at the old price multiplied by the fall in price, shows the amount forgone, while the dotted area, which is equal to the increase in quantity multiplied by the new price, shows the extra amount gained. Sales revenue will increase when the price is reduced provided that the dotted area is larger than the shaded area.[2]

[2]Economists sometimes summarise the argument by using a concept known as *price elasticity,* defined as the percentage increase in quantity sold divided by the percentage decrease in price. It can then be argued that a decrease in price will increase sales revenue if price elasticity is greater than 1, leave sales revenue unchanged if price elasticity is equal to 1 and reduce sales revenue if price elasticity is less than 1. For example, if price elasticity is 1 and price is reduced by, say, 10%, then 10% more units will be sold than before but each of the units will be sold for 10% less than before so that the firm's sales revenue will remain unchanged.

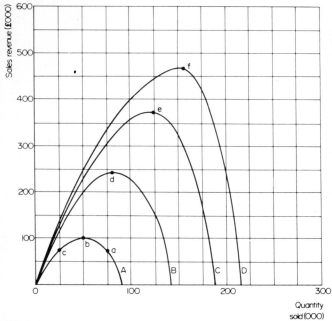

Fig:2.4

Figure 2.2 shows how sales revenue changes as the selling price of the product is changed. Of course, as the selling price changes so the quantity sold alters but quantity sold is not shown explicitly in the figure. It is often more useful to show sales revenue and quantity sold explicitly and to leave selling price implicit. This is shown in Fig. 2.4.[3] Note that the peak in any curve lies to the right of the peaks in lower curves.

[3]The curves shown in Fig. 2.4 are known as *total revenue curves*. Some authors prefer to show *average* and *marginal revenue curves*. Average revenue is revenue per unit and is therefore equal to price. Marginal revenue is the change in revenue resulting from a unit change in quantity sold. Note that around the peak of the total revenue curve marginal revenue is zero as a unit change in quantity sold makes no change to sales revenue, while to the left of the peak marginal revenue is positive and to the right it is negative. This is summarised in the diagram right:

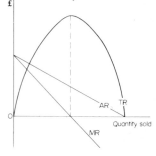

2.3 Revenue and market structure

Before we leave the discussion of the firm's revenue curve and turn to an examination of the relationship between the firm's output and the costs of producing and selling that output, we must consider how the market conditions under which a firm is operating affect its revenue curve. This can be done by considering the structure of the market in which the firm operates. A convenient way of looking at market structure is to draw a distinction between markets where firms are 'searching' for a price that is the 'best' for pursuing a particular objective (*price searchers'* or *price makers'* markets) and markets where the firm has no choice but to accept or 'take' a particular price determined by the market (*price takers'* markets).

There would seem to be little doubt that nowadays more than ever before price searchers' markets are the rule and price takers markets the exception, so we shall begin with an examination of a simple form of price searchers' market and compare it with a price takers' market. After this comparison we shall examine in more detail some other types of price searchers' markets.

One very simple form of price searcher's market is *monopoly*. Monopoly exists if there is a single supplier of a product. In this case the demand curve represents the aggregate behaviour of all the buyers and potential buyers of the product. If the demand curve is downward sloping as in Fig. 2.1 then as price is reduced existing buyers are encouraged to buy more of the product and new buyers are encouraged to switch from some other product to the monopolist's.

Monopoly may be contrasted with a price takers' market which represents a situation of *perfect competition*. Perfect competition is really the other extreme from monopoly. It exists if a very large number of small and independent firms producing an identical product sell to a very large number of independent and unidentified buyers and if, in addition, there are no barriers preventing new firms from setting up or old firms from closing down.

We now have to distinguish between the activities of the individual firms and the activities of the market in which the results of firms' individual decisions are felt. We have to deal here with a system of feedback, for firms' decisions will influence what happens in the market while what happens in the market will influence firms' decisions. To start our argument off we shall assert [and this assertion will be justified in Section 3.3 (ii)] that, as the price at which they can sell their product increases, firms will offer an increasing quantity for sale and hence that each firm has a *supply curve* of the kind shown in Fig. 2.5. Adding together the supply curves of each of the firms gives us the supply curve for the whole market, or the *market supply curve*, as shown in Fig. 2.6. If there is an upward sloping market supply curve and a

Fig:2.5

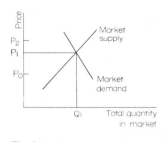

Fig:2.6

downward sloping demand curve then there will be a price at which the quantity offered for sale (*supply*) is exactly equal to the quantity which can be sold (*demand*). This price is P_1 and the quantity offered for sale and sold at this price is Q_1. At other prices supply and demand would not be equal and economists argue that, in most markets, forces operate to establish the price P_1. For example, at a price of P_0 demand would exceed supply. This would mean that a shortage of the good would develop and this would in turn set up a tendency for price to rise to P_1. At a price of P_2 supply would exceed demand. This would mean that a surplus of the good would develop and this would in turn set up a tendency for price to fall to P_1.

If we now turn to the individual firm, we can see that the demand curve which it faces will depend upon market demand and market supply. In perfect competition, the firm is only one of a very large number of firms in the market making an identical product. This means that if it charged a price higher than P_1 it would have no sales as its unidentified buyers would obtain their goods elsewhere at the price P_1. On the other hand, it can sell any quantity it wants without lowering its price below P_1 because any change in its sales will be negligible in relation to the total sales by all the firms and hence it will have a negligible effect on the market price. Hence the firm's sales revenue curve is a straight line whose slope is determined by P_1. This is shown in Fig. 2.7.

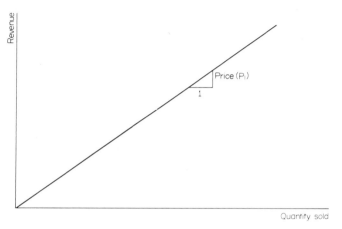

Fig:2.7

Returning now to other forms of price searchers' markets which are less extreme than monopoly, we can distinguish a form known as *oligopoly*. The word oligopoly is, like monopoly, derived from Greek roots and is used to denote a situation in which a few firms produce the whole market supply. However, the existence of 'a few' firms in an industry does not always make it necessary to analyse this market in a special way. For example, there may be six firms operating in a market, with one firm having a market share of 95% while the remaining five firms have a market share of 1% each. In such a situation the giant may be able to ignore the existence of the dwarfs as their pricing policy will have a negligible effect on his situation. The giant can behave as if he were a monopolist and the other firms would be price takers, taking the price set by the giant. In many situations, however, the presence of a few firms in the market induces them to monitor each other's pricing and output decisions and they may well respond to any changes made by a competitor. In such a situation it makes little sense for us to examine the effects of a price cut by one firm while other firms' prices remain constant if the firm can expect such a price cut to be followed by similar cuts made by other firms. Instead we should attempt to incorporate the firm's anticipations as to the other firms' reactions into our model. One very useful way is to use the language of game theory and to regard the firms as a number of players in a game which is won by anticipating the likely moves of the other players.

We shall attempt to describe oligopoly by extending our graphical analysis. We begin by arguing that in some way the firms in oligopoly arrive at prices for their products which are acceptable to them all.[4] These prices might be decided by a deliberate, and sometimes illegal, price fixing agreement or they might just emerge as the generally accepted business practice. Once the prices have been arrived at individual firms must consider the effects of a unilateral change in price. They may well feel that a price rise should be avoided as other firms will maintain the old prices and hence customers will switch away from the firm and its sales revenue will fall drastically. Equally, they may well feel that a price cut should be avoided as if they begin to attract many customers away from other firms these firms will retaliate by cutting their prices as well and hence reducing the price cutter's sales revenue. In a situation like this the individual firm's 'demand curve' and its associated sales revenue curve tend to have a discontinuity or 'kink' around the existing price and quantity combination. We have written demand curve in inverted commas because it differs from the usual curve of economic theory which shows the effect of a change in price when everything else is unchanged. This time we argue that everything else would *not* remain unchanged and try to incorporate into the curve the effects of the other changes which the price change will itself cause. Kinked demand and sales revenue curves are shown in Fig. 2.8.

Finally, in looking at the broad spectrum of price searchers' markets we may have a third important type of market for in many

[4]It is often argued that the price is fixed in such a way that firms with a typical costs structure maximise profits. Hence the firms in the oligopoly get together to act as a monopolist and then to distribute the monopoly profits among individual firms.

Fig:2.8

situations there is a large number of firms selling goods that are more or less alike but for which the customers have their brand preferences. Since we have already borrowed from the Greek language in using the words 'monopoly' and 'oligopoly' we might as well be consistent and add a third: *polypoly*.A polypoly describes a market situation characterised by the existence of a large number of firms which sell differentiated products. As in the oligopoly case the 'polypolist' will not be confronted with the market demand curve. If an individual firm in a polypoly situation lowers its price (and other firms do not) then it may have some effect on the market demand curve if customers feel that the good which it and its competitors produce has now become slightly cheaper on the average relative to other goods. But the major impact of the price change is likely to be on the firm's share of the total market, the share being larger the greater the price advantage of the firm relative to its competitors. Hence it might be argued that the individual firms face 'demand curves' which lie to the left of the market demand curve and which show the share of the market obtained by each of them. It might also be argued that each firm's 'demand curve' will be flatter than the market demand curve because customers can respond to price changes by buying from one firm rather than another without having to make much change in the total quantity which they buy. If the firm faces downward sloping 'demand curves' we can use Fig. 2.4 to represent its sales revenue curves, bearing in mind that the curves now refer to the firm's share of the market rather than to the whole market.

But can we assume that a fairly simple and straightforward relationship between prices and sales volumes exists in the polypoly case? Over a certain price range we may well assume that

Fig:2.9

as prices are changed some customers will be lost or gained (depending on the direction of the price change), but however strong the preferences for one firm's goods are, once a particular price (in relation to the average prices charged by the competing firms) is reached, brand loyalty may become too expensive for its customers and the firm may price itself out of the market and lose all customers. On the other hand, if one firm pursues a price lowering policy there must eventually be a price at which customers lose their loyalty to other firms and would transfer their demand to the price cutting polypolist. Figure 2.9 illustrates the kind of demand and revenue curves the polypolist might be confronted with: this 'double-bend' demand curve[5] suggests that buyers' response to price changes would be significantly different once the polypolist operated outside a particular price range.

2.4 Costs

In this section we shall consider the relationship between the firm's output and the costs of producing and selling that output. We shall conclude that costs increase as output increases. Readers may feel that such a conclusion is so obvious that any further discussion is superfluous, but it will be helpful to introduce some of the material contained in later chapters by examining the relationship between costs and output more closely here. We shall

[5]This particular interpretation of a polypolist's 'demand curve' was first developed by E. Gutenberg in *Grundlagen der Betriebswirtschaftslehre,* 2 Band, Der Absatz, Springer 1955.

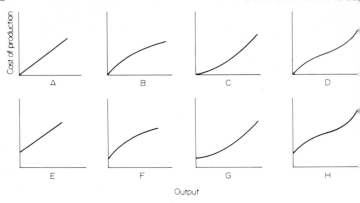

Fig:2.10

do this in terms of the curves shown in Fig. 2.10 which represent possible forms for the relationship between costs of production and output and which are usually known as *cost curves*. Consider first curve A which is a straight line passing through the origin. A firm would have a cost curve of this form if any change in output required a proportionate change in each of its inputs and if it could obtain each of its inputs at a fixed price. Hence, for example, a doubling of its output would need a doubling of its inputs which would in turn lead to a doubling of its costs.

Some firms operate in these conditions but many do not. It is not difficult to think of some reasons why there may not be so simple a relationship between output and costs. The expansion of the firm's labour force may allow greater specialisation of labour with associated increases in productivity. Large outputs may make it worthwhile for the firm to buy specialised capital equipment which may also increase productivity. As the firm increases the size of its order for inputs from other suppliers so it may be able to negotiate discounts or some other special arrangements which reduce the price or increase the quality of its inputs. These considerations would produce a cost curve like curve B. This curve is upward sloping showing that costs increase with output but its slope decreases showing that costs increase less than proportionately to output. Hence a doubling of the firm's output leads to less than a doubling of its costs.

On the other hand, there may be factors at work in the other direction. Managerial control may become increasingly difficult as the size of the firm increases so that the size and cost of the management team has to be increased more than proportionately to output. The workforce may feel that as the organisation grows so it becomes impersonal and this may cause a reduction in productivity. If the firm becomes so large that it is a major buyer in the market[6] for its inputs then any increase in its own demand for inputs might raise the price of those inputs. These considerations would produce a cost curve like C which has an increasing slope showing that costs increase more than proportionately to output. Hence a doubling of the firm's output leads to more than a doubling of its costs.

Studies of firms' cost conditions indicate that many firms have cost curves like curve D. Curve D can be thought of as a combination of curves B and C indicating that as output increases the factors leading to a more than proportionate increase in costs gradually outweigh those leading to a less than proportionate increase.

So far we have used a comparative static presentation and have not introduced any consideration of time and, although we have not stated this explicitly, our discussion of the relationship between costs and output has assumed that firms try to minimise their production costs. (This is known as the *least cost* method.) Now it may take the firm some time to adjust its production process to the least cost method. The implications of this are shown up most clearly by considering the extreme case of zero output. If a firm decides to produce no output then it effectively ceases its operations and exists in name only. The costs of production will then be zero and its least cost curves pass through the origin as do curves A, B, C and D. However a firm which has been producing an output and then decides to produce no output may have to wait for some time before it can dispose of its assets such as its machinery or its office furniture or before it can give up the lease of any rented accommodation and so on.

Similarly, a firm which temporarily produces no output, perhaps because of a strike, does not cease its operations and may

[6]As in the discussion of revenue we find that the structure of the market for inputs crucially determines whether prices vary with the quantity used by the firm.

well incur costs such as rate payments on its buildings and salaries of office staff. Economists describe these costs as *fixed costs* and other costs as *variable costs*.[7] The curves showing the costs of temporarily producing no output may well not pass through the origin and may take forms such as curves E, F, G and H, where the intercept corresponds to the firm's fixed costs.

The same sort of reasoning holds for an increase in output. The least cost method of increasing output may be to take on more labour and to buy more machines but if it takes time to order and install more machines the firm may decide to increase its output initially by increasing its offers of and possibly payments for overtime working. The costs of producing the output might be greater under the overtime system than the least cost method but it may still be a sensible method to use while the new machinery is being put into operation.

To sum up, the faster the firm has to adjust its output the more likely it is that it will be unable to vary some of its inputs within the time period and hence the more likely it is that its costs of production will exceed those of the least cost method. This is illustrated in Fig. 2.11 where the solid curve shows the relationship between output and the least cost method of producing it and the dotted curve shows the relationship between output and costs if the firm adjusts its output more quickly than its input. The firm's input will, however, be just the right amount to allow least cost production of one particular output (q_1) and at this output the two curves touch. If we could observe a firm which suddenly increased its output from q_1 to q_2 then we might find that initially its costs of production were *a* but that as it adjusted its input more fully its costs fell towards *b*.

We shall use a curve such as curve H in Fig. 2.10 to represent the general relationship between the output which is produced and the total costs of producing that output.[8]

[7]Note that these definitions are not the same as accountants' definitions.

[8]As in the case of the total revenue curves, some authors prefer to show *average* and *marginal cost curves*. *Average cost* is cost per unit and *marginal cost* is the increase in cost caused by the production of an extra unit. Total, average and marginal cost curves are shown in the diagram right:

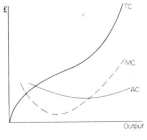

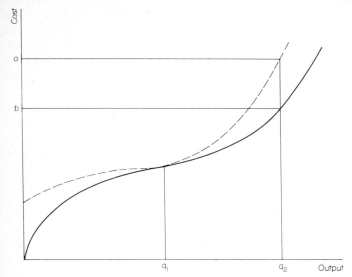

Fig: 2.11

2.5 Costs and revenues

We may now combine the examination of costs and revenue and see the framework in which the firm must take its decisions. This is shown in diagrammatic form in Fig. 2.12 which combines a sales revenue curve of Fig. 2.4, labelled R, with a cost curve of Fig. 2.10, labelled C.

If the decision makers within the firm are presented with data about revenue and costs of the kind represented in Fig. 2.12 they can then decide on the firm's output. What is important for our analysis is that the decision which they make will depend on their objectives. If they wish to make profits then they must choose an output greater than q_1 and smaller than q_2. If they wish to break even they can choose either q_1 or q_2. If they wish to maintain a certain minimum market share corresponding to an output q_{min} then they cannot choose on output smaller than q_{min}.

In terms of the formal expressions introduced in Chapter 1, we can say that the process of decision making involves a comparison between the set of possibilities from which a choice

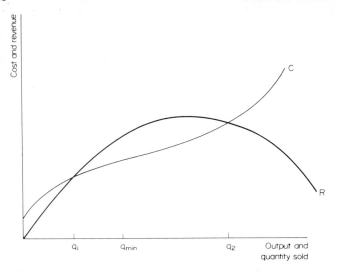

Fig:2.12

can be made, known as *the choice set*, and the objectives to be achieved, known as *the objective function*. This comparison allows the firm to pick from the choice set that possibility which best allows it to achieve its objectives. In general each different objective function will lead to the choice of a different possibility from the choice set.

So far we have outlined the methodology used by economists to analyse problems and have applied the methodology to the problems faced by firms. This has allowed us to derive the firm's choice set. In the chapters that follow we shall show how different objectives lead the firm to select different possibilities from its choice set and from this how firms may react in different ways to changes in their circumstances depending upon their objectives. As far as possible in later chapters we shall base our analyses of firms' behaviour in price searchers' markets on the case of a simple downward sloping demand curve and curved revenue curve. Only when our conclusions differ with the adoption of the special forms of the demand curves which we have discussed shall we refer to different types of price searchers' markets.

Suggestions for further reading

The theoretical approach to the description of the firm's choice set is contained in numerous microeconomics textbooks. Useful ones, arranged in rough order of difficulty, are:

R.G. Lipsey, *Positive Economics,* Weidenfeld and Nicolson 1971.
P.A. Samuelson, *Economics: An Introductory Analysis,* McGraw-Hill 1973.
H. Grayson, *Price Theory in a Changing Economy,* Collier Macmillan 1965.
W.J.L. Ryan, *Price Theory,* Macmillan 1960.
D. Laidler, *Introduction to Microeconomics,* Philip Allan 1974.
K.J. Cohen and R.M. Cyert, *Theory of the Firm,* Prentice Hall 1965.
W.J. Baumol, *Economic Theory and Operations Analysis,* Prentice Hall 1965.

Baumol gives a fascinating introduction to game theory while Cohen and Cyert provide examples of how firms in an oligopoly arrange mutually satisfactory prices.

Interesting discussions on the empirical estimation of a firm's demand, sales revenue and cost curves are contained in:

J. Dean, *Managerial Economics,* Prentice Hall 1951.
D.S. Watson (ed), *Price Theory in Action,* Houghton Mifflin 1969.
J. Johnston, *Statistical Cost Analysis,* McGraw-Hill 1960.
R. Turvey, *Economic Analysis and Public Enterprises,* Allen and Unwin 1971.
G.C. Archibald (ed), *The Theory of the Firm,* Penguin 1971.
J.M. Buchanan and G.F. Thirlby (eds), *LSE Essays on Cost,* Weidenfeld and Nicolson 1973.
L. Wagner and N. Baltazzis, *Reading in Applied Microeconomics,* Clarendon Press 1973.

3
Profit maximisation

3.1 Introduction

In Chapter 2 we showed how the firm can examine the possibilities making up its choice set and outlined how different objectives would lead the firm to make different selections from the choice set. In this chapter we shall examine the implications of having the maximisation of profits as an objective. We shall see how a profit maximising firm would react to changes in its situation so that in the final chapter we can compare these reactions with those which result from other objectives and discuss the possibility of comparing these reactions with those actually observed in the economy in order to find out something about firms' objectives.

3.2 The profit maximiser in equilibrium

The monopolist's cost and revenue situation is shown in Fig. 3.1. As already indicated, the amount which the monopolist chooses to offer for sale will depend on his objectives. On the assumption that he aims to maximise his profits he will choose that output at which total revenue exceeds total cost by the greatest amount. This output is q_{pm}. Note that at this output the two curves have the same slope; at output levels below q_{pm} the curves diverge, showing that the slope of the cost curve is less than that of the revenue curve, while at output levels above q_{pm} they converge showing that the slope of the cost curve is greater than that of the revenue curve.[1]

---

[1]The slope of the cost curve shows the increase in cost incurred when output is increased by one unit, i.e. *marginal cost,* while the slope of the revenue curve

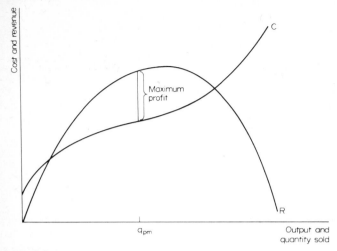

Maximum profit

q_{pm}

Output and quantity sold

Cost and revenue

C

R

Fig:3.1

The situation of the firm in oligopoly is shown in Fig. 3.2. The firm will maximise its profits by choosing the output q_{pm} corresponding to the kink. Now there is not usually a point at which the two curves have the same slope; however, at outputs below q_{pm} the slope of R is greater than that of C, while at outputs above q_{pm} the slope of R is less than that of C so that in a sense the kink represents the point at which they are more nearly equal. It is possible that the firm has a cost curve whose slope increases so rapidly that the point where R and C have the same slope occurs at an output below the kink, in which case it maximises its profits by charging an unusually high price relative to the other oligopolists and producing a correspondingly low output. Such a firm could not be typical of the oligopolists, however, as the kink occurs at the price which maximises the profits of the typical oligopolists! So far our results seem to be similar to the more

---

shows the increase in revenue gained when one extra unit is sold, i.e. *marginal revenue*. This leads some economists to say that the firm wishing to maximise its profits should look at the margin and compare its marginal cost with its marginal revenue and choose that output at which marginal cost is equal to marginal revenue, for if marginal cost is less than marginal revenue (and the revenue and cost curves diverge) profits can be increased by raising output while if marginal cost is greater than marginal revenue (and the curves converge) profits can be increased by reducing output.

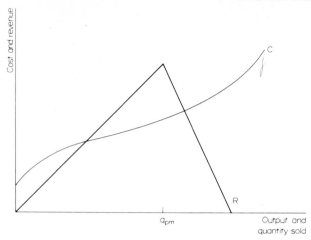

Fig:3.2

general case, but we shall see later that a firm in a situation of
oligopoly may often react to changes in its circumstances in a
rather special way.

The firm in a polypoly situation chooses its price and output
in the same way as the monopolist, by finding the point at which
the revenue and cost curves diverge by the greatest amount.

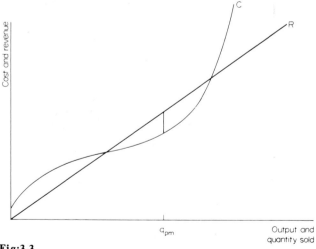

Fig:3.3

The situation faced by a firm in a situation of perfect competition is shown in Fig. 3.3. Despite the difference in shape of the firm's choice set when compared with that faced by a monopolist, the profit maximising output occurs at the point at which the cost and revenue curves have equal slopes and hence are the furthest apart.[2] The only difference between the two situations is that the firm in perfect competition cannot choose its selling price while the firm in monopoly automatically determines a selling price by deciding upon its output. It is for this reason that the firm in perfect competition is known as a price taker.

3.3 Changes in the firm's situation

(i) A shift in the firm's demand curve (market demand unchanged)

The demand curve of a firm in a situation of polypoly or oligopoly may shift even if there is no change in the market demand curve, as there may be a change in people's tastes away from one firm's product and towards another's. Such a situation can occur only in polypoly or oligopoly, as a monopolist is the sole supplier of a product and his demand curve is therefore the market demand curve while a firm in perfect competition produces an output identical to that of other firms and hence people's tastes cannot change between firms.

If people's tastes change in favour of a firm's product its demand curve will shift away from the origin indicating that the firm could command a higher price for the same output. This in turn will shift the firm's sales revenue curve as any level of output will now produce more revenue than before. The general case is given in Fig 3.4(b) which shows that the firm maximises its profit by increasing its output and its prices.[3] The maximum amount of

[2]Strictly, it is necessary to find the output at which the curves have equal slope and at which the revenue curve lies above the cost curve. In the diagram the curves also have equal slopes at a rather low output but here costs exceed revenue and the firm would make a loss, more precisely the maximum loss possible!

[3]It is not obvious from the figure that the firm would raise its price as well as its output. However, if the firm was initially in equilibrium the cost of producing an extra unit was equal to the extra revenue which the sale of that unit would produce. If the firm's cost curve is upward sloping an increase in output without an increase in price would add more to costs than to revenue and the firm would reduce its profits.

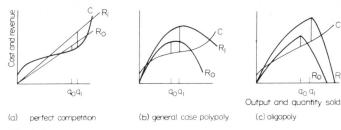

(a) perfect competition   (b) general case polypoly   (c) oligopoly

Fig:3.4

profit is greater in the new situation than in the old. Although this conclusion is generally true it is possible that people's tastes change in such a way that as the firm's demand curve shifts away from the origin its slope also changes so that any price change has a smaller effect on the quantity which can be sold. In such a case the firm may maximise its profits by increasing its price and *reducing* the quantity sold. The effects of such a change in the firm's demand curve are discussed at greater length in Section 4.3 when we consider the possibility that a firm may use advertising to change people's tastes.

The firm (or firms) which finds its demand curve shifting towards the origin as a result of the change in tastes will in general react in the opposite way, that is by reducing its price and its output. Its maximum amount of profit will be reduced by the change.

Assuming that the kink in its demand curve still occurs at the same price, the firm in oligopoly maximises its profits by increasing its output and keeping its price constant, as shown in Fig. 3.4(c), unless the slope of the cost curve increases so rapidly that the cost curve and the revenue curve R_1 have the same slope at an output lower than that corresponding to the kink.

(ii) A change in the number of firms in the market[4]

The market supply curve is the sum of the individual firm's supply curves so that a change in the number of firms will cause a shift in the market supply curve. This in turn affects the remaining firms' sales revenue curves. For example, if the number of firms is reduced the market supply curve will shift to the left. This will raise the price and lower the quantity at which the market

[4]Note that this is impossible in a situation of monopoly.

demand and market supply are equal. Firms in perfect competition will find that as market price rises so their sales revenue curves will swing anticlockwise as shown in Fig. 3.4(a). This will induce them to take advantage of the higher market price by increasing their output and hence their profits. This reasoning provides the justification for the assertion in Section 2.3 that a profit maximising firm in perfect competition would react to a rise in price by increasing its output. The situation in oligopoly is rather more complicated. As we saw in Section (i) the firm in oligopoly tends to keep its price unchanged and to alter its output. It is possible that all firms would do so in this case. However, if the number of firms in the market were reduced and if remaining firms maintained their old prices and increased their output then we know that they would fail to maximise collective profits as we have already seen that a monopolist achieves maximum profits by increasing prices as well as output. This makes it likely that a new collective agreement would be reached under which prices would be raised. This would shift the kink in the new sales revenue curve so that it lay to the right of the kink in the original curve R_0 but to the left of the kink in the absence of a new agreement. A firm now in monopoly or firms in polypoly will find that their sales revenue curves will shift as shown in Fig. 3.4(b) and they will react in the way described in Section (i).

(iii) A shift in the market demand curve

If the market demand curve shifts away from the origin then the equilibrating price at which market demand and supply are equal will rise. The firm in perfect competition will find that its sales revenue curve swings anticlockwise as in Fig. 3.4(a) and will therefore increase its output and profit, while the firm in polypoly will find its sales revenue curve shifting as in Fig. 3.4(b) and will therefore raise its price and increase its output and profit. If the market demand curve shifts towards the origin firms will react in the opposite way, that is the firm in perfect competition will reduce its output and gain a reduced profit while the firm in polypoly will lower price and output and gain a reduced profit.

If firms in oligopoly make no new agreements then an expansion in market demand will induce each firm to increase its output and maintain its price while a contraction in market demand will induce each firm to reduce its output. If the changed

circumstances induce the firms to make a new agreement then
price will also change, moving in the same direction as output.
Some economists argue that a new agreement is more likely in the
case of a demand expansion than in the case of a demand
contraction with the result that the price of a product produced by
a group of oligopolists falls only rarely. This would be the case if
the oligopolists feared a possible price war in which each firm kept
trying to undercut the others with the result that price would
eventually fall below the level which would maximise collective
profits.

Under perfect competition there will be a secondary effect if
the change in firms' profits encourages firms to enter or leave the
market. For example, if the market demand curve shifts towards
the origin firms find that their profits are reduced. If this causes
some firms to leave the market fewer firms are left sharing the
market and the market supply curve will shift to the left. This
induces the results discussed in Section (ii) so that the fall in price
and reduction in profits made by the firms which remain in the
market are smaller than they would otherwise have been.

As discussed in Chapter 2 the freedom of entry and exit which
occurs in perfect competition may encourage so many firms to
leave the market that the effects of their exit offset those of the
original fall in demand so that firms which remain in the market
find themselves facing the same price and selling the same quantity
after the shift in the demand curve as they did before. Some
economists argue that such entry and exit will ensure that firms
which stay in the market never earn more than the minimum
amount of profit which they need to survive (except temporarily
during the adjustment process) and hence all the quantity
adjustment which takes place is due to changes in the number of
firms in the market and hence to shifts in the market supply curve.
The market supply curve itself will still be upward sloping if the
cost of each firm's inputs depends on the total demand for them
generated by all the firms in the market.

(iv) An increase in lump sum taxation

Suppose a lump sum tax is imposed on firms by the
government or that an existing tax is increased. This will shift
every point on the firm's cost curve vertically upwards by an
amount equal to the tax. The profit associated with each level of

output will therefore fall by the same amount. It follows from this that the output which maximised profits before the increase in tax will still maximise profits after the increase, although the size of these profits will be reduced by an amount equal to the increase in fixed costs. Hence, except in the case where the increase in tax is so large that the firm makes losses on its activities, an increase in tax will not cause the profit maximising firm to alter its decisions. This is shown in Fig. 3.5.

If the lump sum tax is imposed on all firms some may decide to cease their operations and drop out of the market in which case the number of firms in the market would change with the effects discussed in Section (ii). These effects will of course be greater the greater the number of firms which decide to cease operations as a result of the tax.

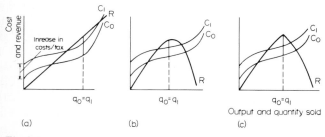

Fig:3.5

(v) Output taxation

If a tax were imposed on each unit of a firm's output then the firm's cost curve would swing anticlockwise for the amount of tax which the firm had to pay would increase as its outputs increased. Such a shift is shown in Fig. 3.6. As before, the firm's choice set is reduced in such a way that the maximum amount of profit which can be obtained is less than before. However, of all the amounts of profits which are now available the maximum amount is not found at the old price and output combination. The firm will maximise its profits after the imposition of the tax by reducing its output and raising its price. As usual the firm in perfect competition is a price taker and hence reacts just by cutting output, while in oligopoly the possibility of other firms' retaliation may induce the firm to

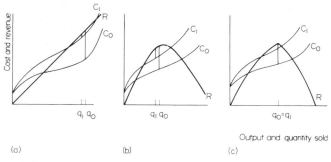

Fig:3.6

take no action and to absorb the tax increase. This is represented by the kink in the total revenue curve which shows that profits are still maximised at the kink even when the cost curve changes its position.

If all firms are subject to the same tax then there may be further repercussions:

(a) It is possible that all the firms in an oligopoly will get together and act like firms in other types of price searchers' markets by agreeing on price rises and output reductions and hence shifting the kink in their sales revenue curves upwards and to the left.

(b) The firm's sales revenue curve is drawn on the assumption that other factors, including the price of similar goods produced by other firms, remain constant (see Section 2.2). If all the other firms in the market raise their prices then the firm's demand curve and its sales revenue curve shift outwards. Hence firms will experience a combination of the situation shown in Fig. 3.6 and that shown in Fig. 3.4. This means that each individual firm reduces its output and raises its price less than it would if it was the only firm to pay the tax. Of course, the effect on the total market is greater as the sum total of the small reductions made by each firm will exceed the large reduction made by a single firm.

(c) If the number of firms in the market falls then the market supply curve will shift to the left, with the results discussed in Section (ii) and this will further enforce the rise in market price and the fall in quantity sold.

(vi) A change in variable costs

If the costs of variable inputs change then the firm's cost curve swings because the size of the change in costs depends upon the output which is produced. The situation is therefore the same as that discussed in Section (v) and the same conclusions follow.

(vii) A change in the firm's fixed costs

As discussed in Section 2.4, the firm may decide to use some inputs in fixed quantities whatever size of output it produces. If so, it will regard the costs of these inputs as fixed. If the price of these inputs increases and if the increase does not induce the firm to reorganise its production process then every point on the firm's cost curve shifts up by an amount equal to the cost increase. Its situation is therefore similar to that following the imposition of a lump sum tax and the same conclusions follow.

It is possible that the increase in the price of inputs that were previously used in fixed quantities would induce the firm to reorganise its production process so as to use less of these inputs and more of the cheaper ones. If so then the situation becomes more complicated. If it found some other input which it also used in fixed quantities the firm's overhead costs would still increase, the size of the increase depending on the price differential between old and new inputs and the efficiency with which the new inputs substituted for the old. However, if the new inputs were also regarded as fixed the firm would not change its price, output or its expenditure on sales promotion. If instead the firm reorganised its production methods so that the old input or its replacements were used in variable quantities then the slope of its cost curve would change and this would cause it to change its output as discussed in Section (vi).

(viii) A rise in profits taxation

If the government imposes a tax on a firm's profits or increases existing rates, this will clearly reduce the amount of profit which firms can retain. Nevertheless, unless the tax rate eventually reaches 100% the firm maximises the amount of profit which it can retain by earning the maximum amount of profits before tax so that the imposition of profits taxation should not induce the profit maximising firm to change its decisions. Even if the tax is imposed on all firms it should cause no change in the number of firms in the market as firms earning no profits pay no tax and so their circumstances are unchanged before and after the imposition of the tax.

(ix) An increase in sales taxation

If the government imposes or increases a sales[5] tax then the firm's revenue after tax is less than its revenue before tax and the difference between the two increases with the amount of revenue. Figure 3.7 illustrates this. R_0 denotes the revenue curve before tax and R_1 denotes the revenue curve after tax. Part (a) shows the situation for the firm in perfect competition whose revenue and hence tax liability increases with output. Such a firm will reduce

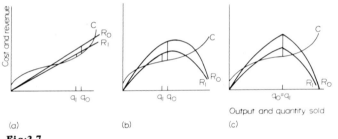

Fig:3.7

its output in order to maximise its after tax profits. Part (b) shows the situation for the firm in a price searchers' market; because sales revenue increases then decreases as output increases so does the firm's tax liability and hence R_0 and R_1 at first diverge then converge. Because R_1 lies below R_0 but also passes through the origin its slope is less at each level of output than the slope of R_0. Hence the profit maximising output at which R_1 and C have the same slope will be less than q_0. The sales tax will therefore induce the firm to reduce its output and to increase its price. Part (c) shows the situation for an oligopolist. If the kink in his sales revenue curve is very pronounced or if the sales tax is small there will be no change in the oligopolist's output and price. A little

[5]A sales tax can be in the form of a unit tax whereby a particular amount is levied on the sales of a good, say 50p, or in the form of a percentage (p.c.) or 'ad valorem' tax. Purchase tax in the UK (abolished in 1972) is a good example of a p.c. tax. For the purposes of our discussion in this and the following chapter we shall assume a p.c. tax; our results would not be altered if we considered a unit sales tax.

experimentation will show that if the kink is not very pronounced or if the tax is large the oligopolist may be induced to reduce his output and to raise his price.

If the tax is imposed on all firms then the change in output and price will have effects on the market as a whole and firms will face a combination of the situation shown in Fig. 3.7 and that shown in Fig. 3.4.

3.4 Summary

The major predictions which have been made in Section 3.3 may be summarised in tabular form (Table 3.1). This will make it

Table 3.1
Objective: profit maximisation

Change in firm's situation	Firm's response:		
	Output	Price	Profits
(i), (ii), (iii) Expansion in demand curve	+	+	+
(iv) Increase in lump sum tax	0	0	−
(v) Increase in output tax	−	+	−
(vi) Increase in variable costs	−	+	−
(vii) Increase in fixed costs	0	0	−
(viii) Increase in profits tax	0	0	−
(ix) Increase in sales tax	−	+	−

0 denotes no change

easier to compare them with the predictions produced from different assumptions about firms' behaviour which we shall obtain in later chapters. However, the reader should bear in mind that the table gives only a summary and many of the prediction have been qualified in the text.

Suggestions for further reading

See any of the microeconomics textbooks listed at the end of Chapter 2.

4
Extensions of the analysis

4.1 Introduction

So far we have used a very simple model to illustrate the firm's choice set and to show how the firm can select a possibility from its choice set according to its objectives. It may seem that the model is so simple that it fails to throw any light on the real problems faced by firms in the economy. In this chapter we shall extend the model and show how a methodology similar to that used in Chapters 2 and 3 can be applied to these more complicated and more realistic situations.

4.2 Price discrimination

In our analysis of pricing decisions we have so far been assuming that firms sell each unit at the same price. Although this is true of a number of situations, there are many cases in which different prices are quoted and charged to different buyers of goods and services, although the goods and services are either identical or virtually identical. One example is the practice on some markets, notably in the Middle East, where buyer and seller bargain individually over the prices for goods. Or we may think of the widespread practice among professionals—doctors and lawyers—to charge relatively high fees to the wealthier patients/clients. Firms may charge different prices for the same or similar goods in different regions (if, say, the degree of competition differs), for example, hi-fi records manufactured in European countries which are sold in the USA at lower prices (despite the transport costs!) than in Europe. And there is considerable variety of price discrimination by sex, age and race t be found. Cinema managers tend to charge different prices t children and old age pensioners (and sometimes to students) o the one hand and members of the 'active' labour force on the othe Producers may exploit the snob appeal of some customers an establish a price difference between goods that is disproportiona' to the quality difference. Supermarkets demonstrate how identic. goods, with different labels attached to them, are offered to th customers at different prices. In the book trade there would appea to be price differences between the hardback and the paperbac editions of books far in excess of the differences in the productic costs incurred for the two editions. Perhaps the best know example of product discrimination is the existence of differenti. prices for public utilities: telephone services and electricity a' cheaper during off-peak times than during peak periods.

That price discrimination is an important feature of busine behaviour is evident from the examples we have just given. Wh. we are, of course, interested in is the question of how busine organisations practising price discrimination (in any of the form we discussed) respond to changes in their situation. But before w can usefully embark on an analysis of this major question, we mu first of all clarify three[1] other important questions:

(a) What precisely constitutes price discrimination?
(b) Under what conditions is price discrimination possible
(c) What advantages does price discrimination offer to firm

The first two questions can be dealt with relatively briefly; a answer to the third will necessitate applying and extending th theory of firms' behaviour developed so far.

How can we define price discrimination? To say tha differences in prices exist for goods and services is obviously n sufficient. For such differences may be accounted for b differences in the cost of production. What we can, broadl speaking, say is that price discrimination takes place whe different units of a good or service are being sold at pric

[1]There is a fourth question arising out of the discussion of pri discrimination that is of vital importance to economics, but which lies outside th scope of this book—is price discrimination socially desirable? Or, more broad speaking, what are the welfare implications of price discrimination?

differentials that do not reflect the supply cost differences between them.

Assuming an employer wants to practise price discrimination, when can he do so? Two conditions would have to be fulfilled to enable a seller to follow a discriminatory pricing policy: first, he must have some control over the price, that is he must be operating in an imperfectly competitive market; second, it must be possible to effectively segregate buyers into groups. If commodities bought at lower prices can be resold from one customer to another, the possibility of price discrimination is undermined if not eliminated.

We now turn to our third and most important question: what advantages does price discrimination offer to firms? For we can safely assume that it is because of its advantages that firms practise price discrimination. We can show that the profit maximising firm can increase its profits through price discrimination, and this is best done by recalling how a non-discriminating profit maximising monopolist fixes his price/output combination.

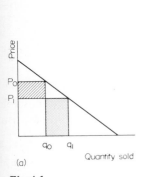 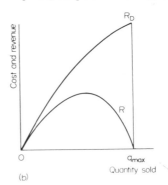

Fig:4.1

Consider the situation of a profit maximising monopolist illustrated in Fig. 4.1. Part (a) of this figure repeats Fig. 2.3 and shows that if price discrimination is not practised a fall in price from P_0 to P_1 will increase quantity sold from q_0 to q_1. This will produce extra revenue shown by the dotted area but will reduce revenue on those units previously sold at a price of P_0 as shown by the shaded area. By comparing these areas one can draw the sales revenue curve (R) of part (b) of the figure. As long as the dotted area is greater than the shaded area, sales revenue will increas with output; when, by lowering the price, the shaded area become greater than the dotted area, the sales revenue will decline - hen the peaked shape of the revenue curve. If the monopolist no practises price discrimination and if he can distinguish betwee units sold then he can avoid losing the revenue shown by th shaded area. This is because he can offer the first unit for sale a a very high price. He then offers a second unit at a slightly lowe price. This either encourages his first customer to buy an extra un or encourages a second customer to enter the market. Now a thir unit is offered for sale at a slightly lower price, and so on. Henc the monopolist gains revenue corresponding to successive dotte areas without losing any corresponding to successive shade areas. The discriminating monopolist's sales revenue will thu always increase with quantity sold up to q_{max} and, at each quanti sold, will exceed the non–discriminating monopolist's revenu This is shown by the curve R_D. Discrimination therefore increase the maximum profit which can be gained.

To determine the profit maximising output the discriminatin monopolist follows the same rule as that already discussed: h considers his cost curve together with his sales revenue curve an chooses the point at which they have the same slope and hence ar separated by the greatest amount. Note that R_D has a steeper slop at every output level than R so that the discriminating monopoli will produce and sell a larger output than the non–discriminatin monopolist.

It is interesting to note that the ability to discriminate ma allow the firm to stay in business when uniform pricing polic would not. Imagine a situation in which the firm's cost curve la above the revenue curve R but below the curve R_D in Fig. 4. Without discrimination the firm would always make a loss on it production, with discrimination profits are possible.

Of course, it is not often possible to distinguish between uni sold although public utilities such as gas and electricity come nea to it by charging a different price for blocks of units such as 2 pence for each of the first 50 units, 15 pence for each of the nex 100, and so on. What is much more common is the ability t distinguish between groups of customers. The more groups whic can be distinguished the greater the opportunities for increase

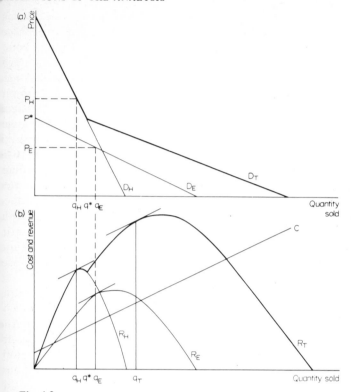

Fig 4.2

profit, but we shall consider the situation where two groups can be distinguished: one group perhaps corresponding to buyers in a home market, the other to buyers in an export market. The firm's choice set in this case is illustrated in Fig. 4.2. Part (a) shows the demand curves in the export and home markets (D_E and D_H). Figure 4.2(b) shows the corresponding sales revenue curves R_E and R_H. The total demand curve (D_T) is found by adding together D_E and D_H; the total revenue curve (R_T) is derived by adding R_E and R_H.[2] The profit maximising output (q_T) is found where R_T and C (the cost curve) have the same slope and hence are separated

[2]In the example chosen D_H is identical with D_T at prices above P^*. Accordingly R_T and R_H are the same up to the output level q^*.

by the greatest amount.[3] The way in which this output is divided
between the two markets is determined by finding the outputs at
which the slopes of R_E and R_H are the same as the slope of C at q_T.
These outputs are q_E and q_H.

To illustrate the way in which this extended analysis can be
used to deal with changes in the firm's situation we shall examine
a question which has been of great interest to observers of
economic policy in the United Kingdom over the last two decades
and has, in particular, given rise to debates between governments
and spokesmen of the motor car industry. The question is - will
a credit restriction on the home market increase exports, reduce
exports or leave them unchanged? As we shall see, the answer
depends crucially on the shape of the industry's cost curve

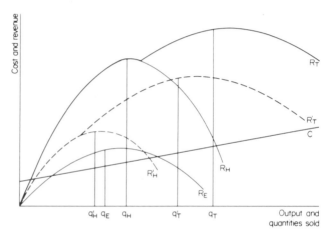

Fig:4.3

A credit restriction has no effect on the export sales revenue
curve but it shifts the home demand curve and hence the home
sales revenue curve to the left from R_H to R'_H in Figs. 4.3, 4.4 and
4.5. Hence, the total sales revenue curve will also change as shown
by the shift from R_T to R'_T. Figure 4.3 shows the result if costs are
proportional to output (i.e. the cost curve is a straight line). Before

[3]In order to keep the diagram as simple as possible, the cost curve C has been
drawn as a straight line. The argument is not changed if it has the more complicated
form used in the earlier diagrams.

the credit restriction profits are maximised at an output q_T, R_E and R_H have the same slope at q_E and q_H respectively as C has at q_T and hence q_E is exported and q_H sold at home. After the restriction the total revenue curve shifts to R'_T and profits are maximised at the smaller output q'_T. Let us see how this reduction is split over the two markets. We note that C has the same slope all along its length. It follows from this that the slope of C at q'_T is the same as its slope at q_T. Hence R_E will have the same slope at q_E as C has at q'_T and so the firm will make no change to its output and sales in the export market. Thus the only effect of the credit restriction is a contraction of the quantity sold and a reduction of the price charged on the home market.

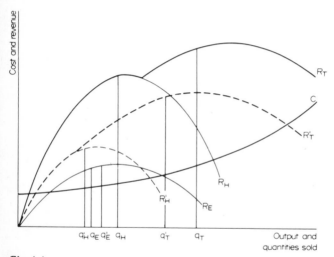

Fig:4.4

Figure 4.4 shows the effect of the credit restriction when costs increase more than proportionally to output. The profit maximising output falls from q_T to q'_T. Now the slope of the cost curve C *increases* with output so that the slope of C is greater at q_T than it is at q'_T. On the other hand, the slope of R_E *decreases* as output rises. Hence, if q_E shows the output at which the slope of R_E is the same as that of C at q_T, then q'_E, which is the output at which the slope of R_E is the same as C at q'_T, will lie to the *right* of q_E That is, the credit restriction at home will lead the firm to increase its export volume and reduce the export price. Similar reasoning about the slopes of R_H and R_H' show that the credit restriction will lead the firm to reduce its sales at home and reduce the price charged on the home market.

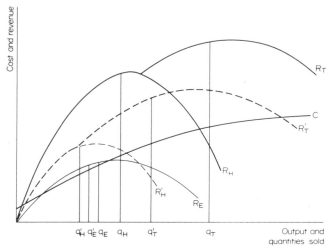

Fig:4.5

Table 4.1
Responses of a (profit maximising) discriminating monopolist to a credit restriction on the home market

Cost conditions	Total output	Home market: Output	Price	Export market: Output	Price
Costs rise more than proportionately	−	−	−*	+	−
Costs rise less than proportionately	−	−	−	−	+
Costs rise proportionately	−	−	−	0	0

*assuming that the home market demand curve shifts rather than swings.

Figure 4.5 shows the effect of the credit restriction when costs increase less than proportionally to output. By arguing in terms of the slopes of the curves the reader should be able to verify that both exports and home sales fall.

Table 4.1 summarises the response of the profit maximising discriminating monopolist to a credit restriction on the home market.

4.3 Advertising

So far, we have not discussed the effects of advertising on our model. If the firm can influence its sales prospects by the amount of advertising which it undertakes, then it may well discover that there is an optimum expenditure on advertising as well as an optimum output. The effect of such advertising on the firm's market can be represented by an outward shift in its demand curve. There are a number of ways in which the demand curve might shift, according to the type of product which is being sold and the type of advertising which is being used. This is summarised in Fig. 4.6. Part (a) shows the result of successive equal increases in advertising expenditure as a general expansion of the market, shown by a shift in the demand curve to the right. After increasing its advertising the firm can maintain the same output and charge a higher price per unit or it can maintain the same price and sell more units or it can increase both its price and its sales. Part (b) shows the result of advertising as a swing in the demand curve from the same point on the quantity axis indicating that advertising has a smaller effect at low prices than at high prices. This might be the result of advertising a product as a prestige item which allows the firm to charge a higher price but does not greatly increase the number of units which can be sold. Part (c) shows the result of advertising as a swing in the curve from the same point on the price axis indicating that advertising has a greater effect at low prices than at high prices. This might be the result of advertising a product as a particularly cheap item so that demand increases as long as the good remains cheap relative to substitutes. Each of the three parts of Fig. 4.6 has been drawn in such a way that successive equal increases in advertising expenditure have decreasing effects on the demand curve as the market becomes saturated with

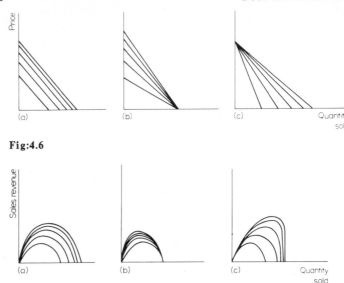

Fig:4.6

Fig:4.7

advertising. This is very often found to be the case in practice although there are some instances in which small amounts of advertising are ineffective so that, as advertising expenditure increases, the demand curve initially shifts by increasing amounts before the process of market saturation sets in and the shifts begin to decrease in size.

The sales revenue curves corresponding to the demand curves of Fig. 4.6 are shown in Fig. 4.7. Part (a) shows the results of an increase in advertising which causes a general market expansion and corresponds to (a) in Fig. 4.6. Each sales revenue curve lies above the preceding one, the vertical difference between each successive curve diminishes and the peak of each curve is found at a greater output than that of the preceding curve. It follows from the first and the last properties that, at any particular level of output, the higher the curve the greater its slope. Part (b) corresponds to (b) in Fig. 4.6. Each sales revenue curve lies above the preceding one, the vertical difference between each successive curve diminishes and the peak of each curve is found at a smaller output than that of the preceding curve. Part (c) corresponds to (c) in Fig. 4.6. These curves are similar to those of (a) except that the peaks of successive curves move to the right more rapidly.

Advertising expenditure will also increase costs so to see how the firm will decide upon its expenditure we must show the costs and revenues associated with different levels of advertising expenditure on a single diagram. This is done in Fig. 4.8 which combines revenue curves similar to those in Fig. 4.7(a) with the typical curve which we have used elsewhere. Figure 4.8 shows that another variable has now entered the firm's choice set for the range of profits which is open to it now depends on the level of advertising. If the firm spends little on advertising then it can make profits, as indicated by the curves R_1 and C_1. If it increases its advertising expenditure then it increases its costs but also increases its revenue, as indicated by the curves R_2 and C_2. If the market becomes saturated with advertising then eventually the increase in revenue will become less than the increase in costs but, as shown in the figure, this need not be the case at lower levels of advertising. To maximise its profits, the firm must now choose

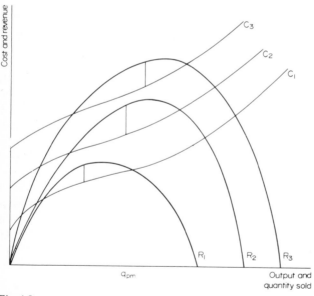

Fig:4.8

the correct output and the correct advertising expenditure. Ignoring curves which lie between those shown in the figure the correct advertising expenditure is that producing curves R_2 and C_2 and the correct output is q_{pm}.

The firm's decision can be explained as in Chapter 3. For each level of advertising the firm must choose the output at which its cost and revenue curves have the same slope, i.e. it must expand its output up to the point at which the extra cost incurred in the production of one extra unit is equal to the extra revenue gained from the sale of that unit. As far as advertising is concerned, then for each level of output the firm must increase its advertising until the extra cost incurred is equal to the extra sales revenue gained from the ability to sell its output at a higher price. As we have already pointed out, both the output and the advertising level must be simultaneously decided as the one affects the other. The greater the level of advertising the greater the output at which the cost and revenue curves have the same slope, while the greater the level of output the greater the increase in revenue which the firm will gain from its ability to sell that output at a higher price.

If there was an expansion in the demand for its product then the firm would revise its decisions accordingly. Suppose for the moment that its advertising budget was fixed and that only its output could be changed. In this case the firm would increase its output and its price in the way described in Chapter 3 and illustrated in Fig. 3.6. The higher output would, however, increase the amount of extra sales revenue which would be generated by an increase in advertising, allowing the firm to sell the output at a higher price. Now if the firm was free to vary its advertising expenditure it would increase this as well, thus shifting the cost and revenue curves; as a result the price and output would rise still further.

It is possible that an increase in advertising always contributes more to costs than to revenue so that the firm never advertises. This is more likely to occur when the firm's output is very similar to that of other firms so that an increase in the firm's advertising expenditure will increase the demand for all the similar goods and only some of this increase will be felt by the firm itself. The extreme case of this is perfect competition in which each of the many firms in the market produces an identical product. Of course, the buyers' views about the degree of difference between goods may depend upon the firm's advertising—skilful advertising may make the buyers feel that there is a large degree of difference so that the firm undertaking the advertising will reap the maximum benefit for itself and give the minimum to its competitors.

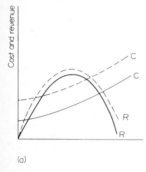 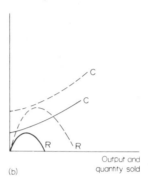

Fig:4.9

We should perhaps point out that our conclusions depend on advertising having the effects indicated in Fig. 4.6(a) or (c). If, instead, advertising has the effect indicated in part (b), the application of our methodology shows that the firm which chooses to advertise at all will maximise its profits by reducing output below the level which maximises profit in the absence of advertising and charging a higher price per unit.

Advertising is sometimes used to prevent new firms from entering the market. This occurs particularly often in oligopoly where a group of firms may get together and agree to act like a monopolist in order to increase collective profits. This may create a threat for them because high profits may encourage new entrants to the market and unless there is some natural or legal barrier to entry the oligopolists cannot prevent this. However, if they advertise they may have little effect on their own sales but they may force a potential competitor to undertake heavy advertising expenditure before his product becomes attractive to the public and this may deter him. This situation is illustrated in Fig. 4.9. The solid lines in part (a) indicate the situation of one of the firms in oligopoly if none of them advertise, while the dotted lines indicate the situation if they all advertise. The solid lines in part (b) indicate the situation of a potential competitor if he does not advertise his product and the dotted lines indicate his situation if he does. It will be seen from the figure that, although the oligopolists make less profit when they advertise than they would if they could stop advertising and still keep the competitor out, they effectively prevent the competitor from entering the market and safeguard their monopoly position.

4.4 Many plants

If the firm operates a number of plants, not all of which are identical, the derivation of its cost curves becomes more difficult as the relationship between costs and output may well differ according to the proportions in which a change in output is distributed across plants. Nevertheless, the same principles apply here as elsewhere. The firm's choice set now involves the method by which it produces its output, as well as other factors like advertising expenditure, and the firm must make its decision by taking account of all the factors simultaneously. To illustrate this process we shall consider the case of a firm which uses two different plants to produce its output.

Such a case is illustrated in Fig. 4.10. C_1 is the cost curve of plant 1 and C_2 shows the cost curve of plant 2. R is the firm's revenue curve, drawn on the assumption that each plant sells an identical product in a single market[4] so that the firm has a single demand curve for the whole of its output. The firm's decision making process can be divided into two parts—first the decision on the proportions in which it divides its total output between its two plants and second, the total output which is to be produced.

When considering the proportions in which its total output will be divided it is clear that if costs increase more than proportionately to output (as in Fig. 4.10) it will always be cheaper to split any output over the two plants than to produce it in a single plant. However, the decision on the proportions in which the split is made is a little more complicated. The firm must look at the costs of changing output by one unit in each plant (marginal costs and divide the total output in such a way that marginal costs are

[4]This assumption allows us to draw a simple diagram but it is not a necessary part of the argument.

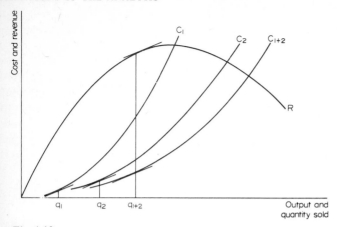

Fig:4.10

equal in each plant. For example, if the marginal cost of production in plant 1 is £6 and the marginal cost of production in plant 2 is £4, the firm can reduce its costs by reducing the output of plant 1 by one unit and increasing the output of plant 2 by one unit, thus saving £2 on its operations while still producing the same output. Such a reallocation between plants will continue to reduce costs until marginal costs are equal in each plant—reducing the output of plant 1 will reduce marginal cost in plant 1 while increasing the output of plant 2 will increase marginal cost in plant 2.

The curve labelled C_{1+2} in Fig. 4.10 shows the cost curve of producing different levels of output when this output is split between plants in the minimum cost way. As the marginal cost of producing any particular output is greater in plant 1 than in plant 2 the split shown by the curve C_{1+2} involves a greater output from plant 2 than from plant 1.

Once the minimum cost production method has been decided upon, the firm can choose the profit maximising output in the normal way. This output, denoted q_{1+2}, is made up of q_1 from plant 1 and q_2 from plant 2. Note that at output q_{1+2} the extra revenue gained from an extra unit sold (marginal revenue) is equal to the extra cost of producing a unit in the optimal way as shown by the slope of the curve C_{1+2}, and that this cost is in turn equal to the marginal cost of producing an extra unit from each of the plants separately. This is indicated by the tangents drawn on the diagram to show that the slope of R at q_{1+2} is equal to the slope of C_{1+2} at q_{1+2} and to the slope of C_1 at q_1 and to the slope of C_2 at q_2.

Figure 4.10 shows a case in which the costs of each plant rise more than proportionately to output. If the firm has a plant whose cost curve is like curves D and H in Fig. 2.10, indicating that at low levels of output costs of production rise less than proportionately to output, then if the firm chooses a low sales volume its costs may be minimised if it produces all its output in this plant and leaves the others idle. At higher sales volumes, which could be satisfied from the plant only if it operated in the range where costs increased more than proportionately to output, the firm would divide its output among all its plants in the way outlined above.

The reader will note that the discussion has been in terms of marginal cost rather than total cost. To minimise its costs the firm has to ensure that the cost of producing one extra unit is the same in each plant. There is no need for the firm to take its fixed costs into consideration when deciding how to allocate its output between plants, but this does not mean that the firm's accountant would not be interested in its fixed costs when assessing its profitability. Indeed, there is a substantial literature dealing with the problem of dividing fixed costs, such as those of the firm's head office, between plants so that the firm can see the profitability of each of its plants.

4.5 Many products

If the firm produces a number of different products the derivation of its cost curves becomes more difficult. If the products are independent in all respects the firm may be able to divide the problem into a number of sub-problems of the kind described above by examining the choice set for each product separately. This is one of the reasons why multiproduct firms often set up a number of divisions each of which covers a product or range of products and can take decisions about production and marketing more or less independently of other divisions. Each division then resembles the single product firm discussed above. In many areas, however, the firm's different activities are not independent. For example, detergent manufacturers often sell a number of similar products under different brand names and an increase in sales of one brand name may well be accompanied by a decrease in sales of another. Hence the firm must consider all its brands together so that its choice set will involve the production and expenditure on sales promotion of each of the brands. It will then make its plans for each of the brands simultaneously.

As an example of dependency through production, consider the refining of crude oil. When crude oil is refined it is possible to change the proportions of petrol, oil, paraffin, and so on which are produced from each unit of crude. Hence, the production costs of one product such as petrol will depend on the production of other oil based products since the greater the proportion of these which are produced the greater the quantity of crude which must be refined in order to produce a certain quantity of petrol. Again, the firm must decide on its plans for each of its products simultaneously.

4.6 The adjustment process

One final problem concerns the way in which the firm adjusts to changes in its situation. This is a consideration which does not appear in a comparative static approach but which will be important when in the final chapter we confront our theoretical predictions with the empirical evidence. If the firm's choice set always remained constant then the problem would not arise but, of course, in practice the firm's choice set keeps changing over time as the costs of its inputs change, as its competitors change their plans, as its customers' tastes change, and so on. Hence the possibility which the firm would like to pick from its choice set will probably keep changing as a result. However, it may be expensive for the firm to change its decisions. For example, if it wants to change its price it has to print new price lists, inform its wholesalers, and so on. If it wishes to expand its labour force it has to advertise the jobs which it offers, interview applicants and possibly retrain its new labour. So if we record the firm's situation at any point in time we may well find that it has not chosen the possibility which we might at first expect. Hence the firm aiming to break even is unlikely to be operating at the *exact* point where its cost and revenue curves

intersect, although it may well always operate near this poi
slowly adjusting to its continually changing circumstances.

A related problem occurs if the firm's actions in one peri
influence its circumstances in later periods. For example, if a fir
decides to spend more on advertising in each year it may find th
the demand for its product increases very little at first but that t
continual advertising has a cumulative effect as more and mo
people become aware of its products, so that eventually demar
rises a lot. If the firm merely compared the cost of the first yea
advertising with the increased sales revenue in the first year
might feel that the advertising was not worthwhile, but if it made
comparison over a longer period it might take a different vie
These considerations mean that the firm may well have to consid
its choice set in a number of periods and to take a decision abo
all these periods simultaneously.

4.7 Summary and outlook

It is important to note that all the complications which w
have introduced change the complexity of the problem rather tha
its nature and for this reason the solution procedure remains t
same. The firm must first take stock of its environment in order t
draw up its choice set and see what possibilities are open to i
Having done this it can pick from these possibilities that whic
best allows it to achieve its objectives. It is because so ma
different problems can be solved with similar procedures tha
economists devote so much attention to the examination of simp
models. When faced with a particular problem the good economi
solves it by breaking it down into parts and noticing t
similarities between the parts and the simple model with which
is familiar. This allows him to draw on his experience of the
models and hence to solve a more complicated problem which ma
at first sight seem intractable. It is for this reason that the followir
chapters deal with different objectives of firms in the context of t
simple model of Chapters 2 and 3 rather than the mo
complicated models of this chapter. Nevertheless, we hope th
readers will be able to decide for themselves how firms wit
objectives other than the maximisation of profits would behave i
each of the five more complicated situations introduced in th
chapter.

Suggestions for further reading
Price discrimination .

ï.S. Becker, *The Economics of Discrimination,* University of Chicago Press 1957.
..C. Battalio and R.B. Ekelund, Output change under third degree discrimination, *Southern economic journal,* October 1972.
. Machlup, Characteristics and types of price discrimination, in *Business Concentration and Price Policy,* National Bureau of Economic Research, 1955
.R. Ball, Credit restrictions and the supply of exports, *Manchester School,* May 1961.

Advertising

. Simon, *Issues in the Economics of Advertising,* University of Illinois Press 1970.
ï. Schmalensee, *The Economics of Advertising,* North Holland 1972.

Many Plants

). Patinkin, Multiple-plant firms, cartels and imperfect competition, *Quarterly Journal of Economics,* February 1947.

Many Products

. Agarwala, Price policy in a multiproduct firm: a case study, *Applied Economics,* August 1969.
..W. Pfouts, Some cost and profit relationships in the multi-product firm, *Southern Economic Journal,* January 1973.

5
Output maximisation

5.1 Introduction

A different hypothesis about firms' behaviour which is sometimes put forward is that they try to attain the largest volume of output and sales which is compatible with a target profits figure expressed sometimes as a target *amount* of profits (with declining unit profit as output increases) and sometimes as a target *rate* of profit on each unit sold.[1] This is sometimes put forward as a special hypothesis about the behaviour of nationalised industries which the public does not expect to maximise profits and which are often set target rates of profit by the government; but it is also sometimes put forward as a general hypothesis about the behaviour of firms.

The introduction of a target profits figure is very important as the maximisation of output without a profits constraint would clearly be an unlikely objective as output could then be increased until total revenue was zero ! Clearly such an increase in output would result in losses and the firm could not survive. The maximisation of output subject to a profit constraint, on the other hand, would seem a plausible goal governing business behaviour and we shall now examine the implications of such an objective on the firm's behaviour.

[1] In the literature the output maximisation hypothesis is often wrongly referred to as full-cost principle, costing plus, etc. To say that firms would want to cover their costs including a certain mark-up is, however, merely stating the obvious and by no means implies what goal firms may be pursuing. A minimum profit is a constraint whatever objective function governs business behaviour. Costing plus is a procedure of pricing, not a description of a goal. For a discussion of this misunderstanding see, for example, A.E. Kahn, Pricing objectives in large companies: comment, *American Economic Review*, September 1959.

60

5.2 Comparison with profit maximisation

It is possible that the firm's situation is so unfavourable that the maximum amount of profit which it could possibly gain is less than or equal to the firm's target. If this is so then the profit maximising firm and the output maximising firm would each choose to produce the same output. If, however, the situation was more favourable and the maximum possible amount of profit exceeded the target amount then the output maximising firm would be prepared to lower its price, increase its output and to accept profits lower than the maximum until profits had fallen to the target amount. This is summarised in Fig. 5.1 which compares the profit maximising output, q_{pm}, with the output maximising output, q_{om}, for a firm in monopoly or polypoly. Part (a) shows the case where the firm wishes to achieve a certain amount of profit, as shown by the line DE, while part (b) shows the case where the firm wishes to achieve a certain rate of profit on each unit sold. q_{om} will never be less than q_{pm}; it will be greater than q_{pm} if the cost plus profit curve cuts the total revenue curve to the right of the point A and it will be equal to q_{pm} if the cost plus profit curve touches A.

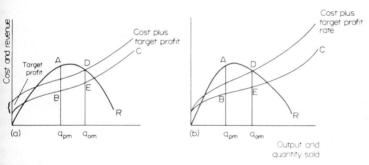

Fig:5.1

A similar argument can be applied to the cases of perfect competition and oligopoly, by drawing sales revenue curves of appropriate shape. As discussed in Chapters 2 and 3, freedom of entry and exit may ensure that the firm in perfect competition can gain only enough profit to allow its survival, in which case the profit maximising output and the output maximising output will be identical. A little experimentation will show that the more pronounced the kink in the oligopolist's sales revenue curve, the smaller the difference between the output maximising and the profit maximising output. Provided such action allows it to satisfy its profit constraint the output maximising firm in oligopoly will charge a price lower than its rivals. Of course, if all the firms in the oligopoly have similar cost and revenue curves and are output maximisers then, since every firm will attempt to reduce prices below those corresponding to the kink, the kink itself will move until it is found above the output maximising output.

5.3 Changes in the firm's situation

As in Chapter 3 we can now analyse the response of the output maximising firm to changes in its situation. As already outlined above, if the situation is so unfavourable that the firm is unable to reach its target profit it will act in the same way as the profit maximising firm so we shall assume here that the situation is such that the target profit could be exceeded if the firm so desired. We shall further deal with cases in which the firm has a target value for *total amount* of profits. The reader should verify that our conclusions remain unchanged if instead the firm has a target value for its *rate* of profit.

(i) An expansion in one firm's sales revenue curve (market demand unchanged)

Such an expansion might come about as a result of a change in customers' tastes away from a rival's product and towards the firm's.[2] This situation is shown in Fig. 5.2. The curve labelled C+Z shows the firm's cost curve plus the target amount of profit. In both polypoly and oligopoly, the expansion in the firm's sales revenue curve induces it to increase its price and output.[3] Because we assume that the firm takes decisions so that it just achieves a target amount of profit, its profit will be the same before and after every change discussed in this chapter. Had we assumed that the firm took decisions so that it just achieved a target *rate* of profit on each unit sold then its profits would be proportional to its output.

[2] As pointed out in Chapter 3, this case cannot arise in perfect competition or monopoly.

[3] If its cost curve is upward sloping, an increase in output that was not accompanied by a rise in price would reduce the firm's profits below the target amount, as argued in footnote 3 of Chapter 3.

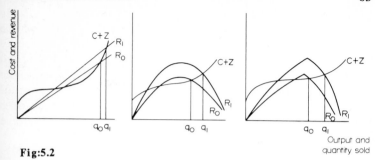

Fig:5.2

(ii) A fall in the number of firms in the market

This will cause a leftward shift in the market supply curve and will raise the price and lower the quantity at which market supply and market demand are equal. Of the firms which remain, those in perfect competition will find that their sales revenue curves swing anticlockwise as shown in Fig. 5.2 and they will increase their outputs accordingly. Those in polypoly will raise both price and output while those in oligopoly will raise output unless they make a new agreement, in which case they will raise output rather less but raise prices as well.

(iii) An increase in market demand

This will raise the price and the quantity at which market supply and market demand are equal. The situation can still be represented by Fig. 5.2. Firms in perfect competition will increase output, those in polypoly will increase output and price, and those in oligopoly will increase only output if they make no new agreement and output and price if a new agreement is reached. If the increase in market demand encourages new firms to enter the market then the effects discussed in Section (ii) will be felt, but acting in the reverse direction.[4]

[4]There is now some doubt about why new firms may be encouraged to enter the market. If all other firms aimed to maximise profits then they would see the possibility of earning increased profits and would enter the market. The reader should verify that in this case an output maximising firm would find its opportunities for making profits so restricted that its decisions would be the same as those of a profit maximising firm. However, if all firms were output maximisers then their actions would always reduce profits to the minimum required level and so profit opportunities would not appear to encourage new entrants. Possibly output maximising firms would be encouraged to enter if they saw existing firms making increases in output.

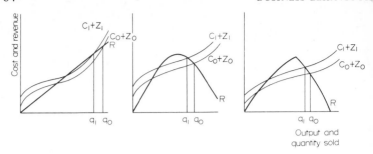

Fig:5.3

(iv) An increase in lump sum taxation

Figure 5.3 shows the firm's situation before and after an increase in lump sum taxation. The curve $C_1 + Z_1$ shows costs plus the amount of profit that must be earned before tax to yield Z_0 after tax. The figure shows that, assuming the firm has in mind an after-tax profit target (rather than a pre-tax target), it will react by reducing its output and increasing its price. The exceptions are the firm in oligopoly, in which case it will reduce its output and increase price only if a new agreement is reached, and the firm in perfect competition which has no direct control over its price.

If all firms faced the same increase in taxation then, as usual, there are further repercussions;

    (a) If some firms cannot survive in the new situation the effects discussed in Section (ii) will also be seen, but acting in the reverse direction.

    (b) The effects of all firms reducing their output will shift each firm's sales revenue curve so that each will face a combination of the situation shown in Fig. 5.3 and that shown in Fig. 5.2.

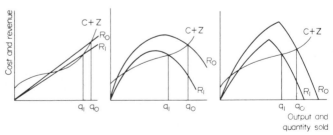

Fig:5.4

(v) An increase in output taxation

This will swing the C + Z curve upwards in such a way that the difference between the old and new curves increases with output. No diagram is shown for this case as it is the intersection of the cost and revenue curves, rather than their slopes, which is important and it is clear that after such a swing the intersection will occur at a lower output and a higher price than before it.

(vi) An increase in variable costs

The results of this will be the same as those of the increase in output taxation discussed in (v).

(vii) A rise in fixed costs

If firms continue to use fixed inputs then they will react to a rise in their price in the same way as they react to an increase in lump sum taxation. If they switch to variable inputs then they will react in the way discussed in Section (v).

(viii) A rise in profits taxation

If firms aim for a target after-tax profit and if they arrange their output and price such that they only just gain this profit, then a rise in profits taxation will have the same effects as a rise in lump sum taxation and the discussion of Section (iv) applies.

(ix) An increase in sales taxation

The effects of an increase in sales taxation are shown in Fig. 5.4. The curve labelled R_0 shows the firm's revenue curve before the change and that labelled R_1 shows the curve (after tax) after the change. A firm in each type of market structure will be induced to reduce output and if not in perfect competition it will also raise its price.

If all firms face the same increase then each will face a combination of the situation shown in Fig. 5.4 and that shown in Fig. 5.2.

5.4 Summary

As in Chapter 3 we have summarised our major conclusions in a table (Table 5.1). The reader should bear in mind that many of the conclusions presented in the table have been qualified in the text.

Table 5.1
Objective: output maximisation

Change in firm's situation	Firm's response: Output	Price
(i), (ii), (iii) Expansion in demand curve	+	+
(iv) Increase in lump sum tax	−	+
(v) Increase in output tax	−	+
(vi) Increase in variable costs	−	+
(vii) Increase in fixed costs	−	+
(viii) Increase in profits tax	−	+
(ix) Increase in sales tax	−	+

Profits remain unchanged throughout

Suggestions for further reading

R.L. Hall and C.J. Hitch, Price theory and business behaviour, *Oxford Economic Papers,* May 1939.
P.J.D. Wiles, *Price, Cost and Output,* Blackwell 1961. (Especially Chapters 4-6.)
E. Ames, *Soviet Economic Processes,* Irwin 1965. (Especially pages 50-66.)
M.J. Kafoglis, Output of the restrained firm, *American Economic Review,* September 1969.

6
Sales revenue maximisation

6.1 Introduction

So far we have analysed firms' reactions to changes in their situations, such as variations in the number of firms, in demand, in costs and in taxation, on the assumption that the firms are attempting to maximise either profit or output—subject always to a profit constraint. A third type of maximising behaviour has been suggested by the American economist W.H. Baumol: that business organisations are interested in maximising the total revenue resulting from sales. As in the output maximisation model, substituting profit maximisation for another objective does not mean that profits become irrelevant. If sales revenue is to be maximised what is meant is that firms, while attempting to achieve the highest possible level of total revenue, nevertheless aim at earning a minimum profit. In other words we are dealing with the notion of sales revenue maximisation subject to a profit constraint.[1]

Why should we assume that firms might strive after maximum sales levels? And if there are grounds for advancing this hypothesis, does this mean that this hypothesis supersedes the profit maximisation assumption?

A number of reasons may be put forward for believing that sales revenue maximisation is a plausible goal underlying business behaviour. It can be argued that for firms operating on price

[1]As pointed out in Chapter 5 (Section 5.1), the profit constraint may be expressed as a target amount of profit or a target rate of profit on each unit sold. We shall assume that firms are interested reaching a target amount of profit; the conclusions we shall draw from our analysis will, however, not be affected if one assumed that firms want to reach a target rate of profit for each unit sold.

searchers' markets there is no *a priori* reason why profits are an end in themselves. The divorce of ownership and management (a characteristic feature of modern business) makes it possible for business organisations to adopt maximum sales as the goal governing their decisions. Sales revenue maximisation would also seem a plausible target of business behaviour in view of the tendency of businessmen to measure the relative success of the firm in terms of its market share. As long as profits are high enough to keep the shareholders content and contribute to the necessary funds for promoting the growth of firms, managers may be determined to increase sales revenue rather than the size of profits. Baumol's justification of sales revenue maximisation as an objective function may have been influenced by his knowledge of American business; the reason he quotes can, nevertheless, claim a certain degree of generality.

Declining sales may have all sorts of disadvantages for a firm: consumers may interpret them as a fall in the popularity or quality of the product the firm sells. Figures indicating falling sales may make it more difficult for firms to obtain credit facilities from their banks or raise finance from the money market generally. Falling sales may also lead to a setback in the marketing system the firm has set up – the firm may lose distributors. A declining sales level in comparison with other competing firms may lead to a reduction in the market power the firm may have established and may want to maintain if not increase. Business executives may be more interested in maximising sales, not only because increasing sales are regarded as a measure of success, but also because this success may be reflected in the salaries and perks they receive.[2] But while firms may be interested in promoting their sales this is not necessarily in conflict with attempts to maximise profits. The

[2]According to one American study, there would seem to be a greater correlation between managers' salaries and the scale of the sales operation of their firm than between salaries and profits. See J.W. McGuire, J.S.C. Chiu and A.O. Elbing, Executive incomes, sales and profits, *American Economic Review,* September 1962. Another study based on US data has shown that increasing sales lead to increasing profits. See B.D. Mabry and D.L. Siders, An empirical test of the sales maximisation hypothesis, *Southern Economic Journal,* Jan 1967. This may make Baumol's hypothesis more plausible; it may, however, also mean, as Peston has argued, that 'if profits in later periods are a function of revenue in the present, the firm in maximising long-run profits will not necessarily simultaneously maximise short-run profits'. (M.H. Peston, On the sales maximisation hypothesis, *Economica,* May 1959.)

strategy of sales promotion, just like attempts to reduce the costs of the business operation, may be nothing but a means to achieve maximum profits. Sales revenue maximisation does, however, become a substitute for or an alternative to profit maximisation if sales 'become an end in and of themselves'.[3]

There are, then, many reasons why sales maximisation would appear to provide us with a plausible hypothesis of business behaviour; we need, however, no longer dwell on the rationale for choosing this objective. As we argued earlier, the validity of this goal of business behaviour (just like the relevance of any other objective we care to include in our theory of the firm) must be judged in the light of the predictions it produces. In other words, whether or not we are prepared to accept sales maximisation as a meaningful substitute for profit maximisation will largely depend on the insight it gives us in our analysis of the response of firms to changes in their situations. If by assuming sales revenue rather than profit maximisation we can explain features of business behaviour more successfully, then the choice of this alternative to profit maximisation would enrich our analysis of the response of firms to environmental changes.

However, before we are in a position to show how sales maximising firms absorb and react to changes in the structure of costs, demand, taxation, etc., we must first of all ascertain what level of output, price and advertising a sales maximiser would aim at in equilibrium and how his decisions would compare with the values of output, price and advertising the profit maximiser would settle on in equilibrium conditions.

6.2 The Baumol model

Figure 6.1 presents Baumol's basic sales revenue maximising model. In the figure, R is the firm's total sales revenue curve, C is its cost curve and Z is its total profit curve found by subtracting C from R. While profits would reach their maximum at the output level q_{pm}, sales revenue is being maximised at the output level q_{sm}. If they were sales revenue maximisers, firms would produce an output level q_{sm}, provided that the profits generated by this output level were satisfactory. If the managers had to earn higher profits,

[3]W.J. Baumol, *Business Behaviour, Value and Growth,* Harcourt Brace Jovanovich 1967 (p46).

say OA, then the sales maximisers' output would be reduced an(
the managers would have to settle for the lower output level q^*_{sm}
Only at this output level would they be in a position to ear(
sufficient profits to meet their target. Clearly, the higher th(
minimum profit figure the business managers have to accept, th(
more important the constraint becomes and the profit maximising
and the sales maximising output levels will be closer together
If—to take the extreme case—minimum profit constraint an(
maximum attainable profit were the same (OB) there would be n(
difference between profit maximising and sales maximising behaviour in terms of the choice of the optimal level of output.

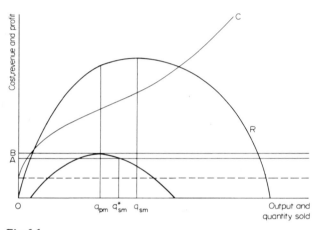

Fig:6.1

Figure 6.1 deals with the general case of a price searchers
market, but the analysis can easily be extended to cover perfec(
competition. In perfect competition the choice set changes shap(
as the sales revenue curve becomes a straight line, but the analysi(
is otherwise unchanged. The particular case of oligopoly is show(
in Fig. 6.2.[4] Total revenue (R) reaches its maximum value at th(
level of output where the kink in the demand curve occurs. Unde(
these circumstances q_{pm} and q_{sm}, the profit and sales maximising
output levels, coincide; the firm would not tend to choose a dif-

[4]In the following analysis we have drawn on ideas first developed b(
W.G. Shepherd, On sales maximising and oligopoly behaviour, *Economica*
November 1962.

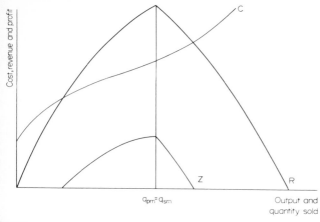

Fig:6.2

erent output level if governed by sales maximising rather than profit maximising behaviour. The kink may of course be less pronounced than the one depicted in Fig. 6.2, in which case the profit and sales maximising output levels need not be identical; they would, however, be closer together than in the case of a straight-line downward sloping demand curve, i.e. in situations with no oligopolistic interdependence in pricing decisions.

An interesting question that arises from the sales revenue maximisation model is how a firm would react if, in a given period of time, the realised profits were higher than the profit constraint. This would occur when the output level for maximum sales revenue is reached before the output level required to meet the profit constraint. (This would be the case in Fig. 6.1 if the profit constraint was as shown by the dotted line.) If sales revenue maximisation is to provide an alternative to the profit maximisation hypothesis, then it must mean *long-run* sales revenue maximisation. Profits in excess of the minimum would clearly enable the firm to take measures conducive to increasing sales, for example further sales promotion. The effects of expenditure on sales promotion or advertising can, as we argued in Section 4.3, be represented as an outward shift of the firm's demand curve.

A simple diagram may serve to illustrate how the choice of a

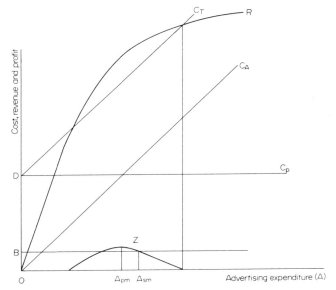

Fig:6.3

firm's outlay on advertising depends on the objective pursued
Assume we measure the level of advertising expenditure on the
horizontal axis in Fig. 6.3 and the revenue and costs on the vertical
axis. At the risk of over-simplifying the issues involved in this kind
of analysis the following assumptions are made:

(i) that increased advertising expenditure always leads to
shifts of the demand curve in the way shown in Fig. 4.6(a) and
(c);
(ii) that successive shifts become smaller if the increases in
expenditure remain equal.

The shape of the revenue curve R follows from our first
assumption: that increased advertising expenditure always
increases revenue, but that the marginal revenue resulting from
additional outlay on advertising diminishes.

Once advertising is introduced into the model we can be sure
that the sales revenue maximising firm will continue to advertise
until its profit constraint is binding. This may be seen by referring
back to Fig. 4.8. In this figure we assumed that the profit maximi

ing expenditure gave rise to the curves R_2 and C_2. If the firm increases its advertising beyond this point it can obtain greater sales revenue as successive revenue curves lie above the preceding ones. Hence in order to maximise sales revenue the firm will go on advertising until advertising increases costs so much relative to revenue that the firm's profit constraint becomes binding. This is shown by the combination R_3 and C_3 in Fig. 4.8. An alternative way of demonstrating this point is shown in Fig. 6.3.[5] The cost curve in this figure is made up of two components - (i) production and distribution costs and (ii) advertising costs. The advertising cost curve C_A is a 45 degree line which is obtained by transferring the figures on advertising expenditure from the horizontal to the vertical axis. Production and distribution costs associated with the firm's output are shown by the line C_P. The total cost curve C_T can then easily be derived by adding up vertically the production and distribution costs C_P and advertising costs C_A. Subtracting the total cost curve C_T from the revenue curve R we can derive the profit curve Z, which now expresses profit as a function of advertising.

What then are the implications of alternative objective functions for the choice of the advertising budget? Faced with identical cost and revenue situations the profit maximiser would choose the advertising expenditure level A_{pm}, whereas the sales maximiser would opt for an advertising budget A_{sm} (given a minimum profit level of the magnitude OB). At a higher minimum profit level the sales maximiser's advertising budget would of course be lower. We see again in this context that the profit constraint on advertising expenditure will always be binding as we have assumed that total revenue continually increases as advertising expenditure is increased and hence has no maximum value. If advertising is always effective in stimulating demand for a firm's products then, of course, with increased advertising the firm would be able to sell higher quantities of its output and usually at a higher price.

Having introduced advertising into the model, we are now in a position to draw more general conclusions and compare them with those we derived from the profit maximising model:

[5]For simplicity we shall use straight lines to represent cost curves throughout the rest of this chapter.

(i)   the sales revenue maximiser will usually produce
higher (and never a lower) output than the profit maximiser
(ii)   he will normally spend more (and never less) o
advertising than the profit maximiser,
(iii)   the higher the level of advertising, the higher the outp
the sales revenue maximiser will produce and sell,
(iv)   the profit constraint will always be binding.

6.3 Changes in the firm's situation

In Chapters 3 and 5 we analysed the response of the profit an
output maximising firm to changes in its situation brought abo
by changes in the revenue or cost side or in the level of taxatio
We shall consider the same kind of changes and attempt to predi
how the sales revenue maximising firm can be expected to respon
to them. We shall, however, simplify our analysis by restricting t
discussion to the case of a simple downward sloping demand curv
and curved revenue curve. The interested reader may neverthele
want to find out on his own whether by considering the 'kinked'
'double bend' demand curves (or even perfect competition
different predictions would emerge.

*(i) An expansion in the firm's demand curve (market deman
unchanged)*

In Fig. 6.4 we show the choices a sales revenue maximize
would make before and after an expansion in his demand curv
takes place. Since we assume that the firm uses both price an
non-price competition, we can argue that before the increase i
demand the firm would have gone on advertising until the prof
constraint became binding. Confronted with the revenue curve R
and the cost curve C our firm would therefore choose the outpu
level q_0. The expansion in the firm's demand curve brings abou
an outward shift of the revenue curve, say from R_0 to R_1. Give
the minimum profit constraint of MP, our firm would respond t
the increase in the demand for its products by producing an
selling the higher quantity q_1: the increase in demand will make
worthwhile for the sales revenue maximiser to raise output an
price. In the case illustrated in Fig. 6.4 we find that at the new ou
put level q_1 the actual profit made by the firm exceeds the min
mum profit, MP. The firm is likely to respond to this situation c

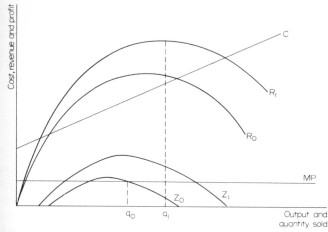

Fig:6.4

'xtra' profits by increasing its sales promotion budget until adver-
ing increases costs so much relative to revenue that the firm's
ofit constraint becomes binding again.

(ii) A fall in the number of firms in the market

Unless we assume that one of the remaining firms experiences
change in the customers' tastes away from its products to those of
e other firms, we would find that the behaviour displayed by the
les revenue maximising firm in response to a reduction in the
umber of firms competing for the sales of a particular type of
ood or service will be the same as that described in Section (i),
nce the firm would benefit from an outward-shifting sales
venue curve.

(iii) An increase in market demand

In this case all the firms in the market experience an outward
ift of their sales revenue curves. Accordingly, all firms will
crease output and raise prices, as shown in Fig. 6.4.

(iv) An increase in lump sum taxation

In Fig. 6.5, before the imposition of the lump sum tax, the firm
ould settle for output q_0. The lump sum tax shifts the total cost
rve from C_0 to C_1 and correspondingly the profit curve from Z_0
Z_1. Under the circumstances, at output level q_0 profits would fall

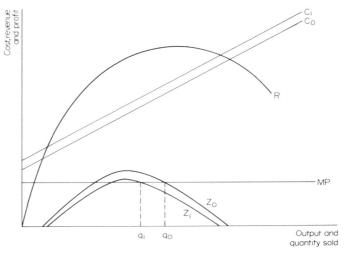

Fig:6.5

below the minimum level, MP. Output would have to be reduced to q_1 in order to reach the level MP again. With the reduction of output, a higher price will be charged.[6]

(v) An increase in output taxation

The change in circumstances brought about by an increase in output taxation would be that the cost curve C in Fig. 6.1 would swing upwards in such a way that the difference between its old and new positions would increase with the level of output. With a higher cost curve the firm's profit curve would be lowered and, given the profit constraint, the sales revenue maximiser would be forced to lower his output level.[6]

(vi) An increase in variable costs[7]

The results of this change in circumstances would be the same

[6]It may be argued that the sales revenue maximiser, in response to increased lump sum or output taxation, adjusts his expenditure on advertising. Such a response is very unlikely, since it would eventually lead to a downward shift of the firm's revenue curve so that the firm would achieve a lower revenue level at any output. Advertising would only be reduced if the firm could no longer achieve the minimum profit at any output level while keeping expenditure on sales promotion fixed.

[7]We have again ignored the possibility of the sales revenue maximiser reducing his expenditure on advertising in response to the various changes in the firm's situation discussed in Sections (vi), (vii), and (ix).

as those we derived for the increase in output taxation in Section (v).

(vii) A rise in fixed costs

In the short run, firms are likely to continue to use fixed inputs and they will, therefore, react in the same way as they would when faced with a lump sum tax. In the medium or long run, firms can be expected to switch to variable inputs and under these circumstances the increase in total costs will be lower. It follows that the reduction in the level of production would be smaller in the long and medium term than in the short term.

(viii) A rise in profits taxation

The reaction to changes in the rate of profits taxation is shown in Fig. 6.6. The profits curve Z_0 shows the behaviour of profits before the change and the curve Z_1 shows the behaviour of after-tax profits after the change. If MP is the required level of profits after tax, then before the increase q_0 is the best output level. After the increase the sales maximiser's response will be to lower his output level and opt for q_1.

(ix) An increase in sales taxation

A sales tax would flatten the (net) revenue curve and this would result in a lower profit curve. The sales revenue maximising

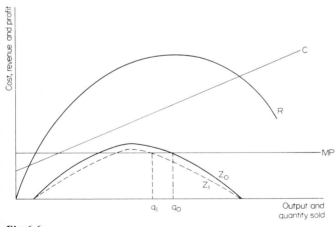

Fig:6.6

firm would have to lower its output (and raise its prices) in an
attempt to maintain the minimum profit level.

Table 6.1
Objective: sales revenue maximisation

Change in firm's situation	Firm's response: Advertising	Output	Price	Sales Revenue
(i), (ii), (iii) Expansion in demand curve	+	+	+	+
(iv) Increase in lump sum tax		−	+	−
(v) Increase in output tax		−	+	−
(vi) Increase in variable costs		−	+	−
(vii) Increase in fixed costs		−	+	−
(viii) Increase in profits tax		−	+	−
(ix) Increase in sales tax		−	+	−

6.4 Summary

The predictions about firms' behaviour in responding to the
various changes in their circumstances have again been
summarised in tabular form (Table 6.1). As for profit
maximisation and output maximisation, if a change in, say,
taxation causes the firm to change its decisions on output then the
imposition of a similar change on all firms will have a primary

effect in the way described above and a secondary effect through the market which will cause all firms' sales revenue curves to shift in the way discussed in Section (iii). The reader should again bear in mind that some of the predictions which have been summarised in the table are qualified in the text.

Suggestions for further reading

W.J. Baumol, *Business Behaviour, Value and Growth,* Harcourt Brace Jovanovich 1967.

M.H. Peston, On the sales maximisation hypothesis, *Economica,* May 1959.

R.L. Sandmeyer, Baumol's sales maximisation model: a comment, *American Economic Review,* December 1964.

W.G. Shepherd, On sales maximising and oligopoly behaviour, *Economica,* November 1962.

C.J. Hawkins, On the sales revenue maximisation hypothesis, *Journal of Industrial Economics,* April 1970.

R.L. Sandmeyer and F.G. Steindl, Conjectural variations, oligopoly and revenue maximisation, *Southern Economic Journal,* July 1970.

R.D. Mabry, Sales maximization vs. profit maximization: are they consistent? *Western Economic Journal,* March 1958.

R. Havemann and G. de Bartolo, The revenue maximization oligopoly model: a comment, *American Economic Review,* December 1968.

7
Managerial utility

7.1 Introduction

So far, we have examined firms' reactions to changes in their circumstances on the assumption that they have a single objective—the maximisation of profits or of output or of sales revenue.

Many economists argue that firms do not have a single objective and that managers weigh up a number of factors when making their decisions. They go on to construct a number of *managerial models* of business behaviour and there are a number of such models of the firm in existence.[1] We shall concentrate on the model developed by the American economist O.E. Williamson as this model seems to be more rigorously defined than many of the others. However, before examining Williamson's model in detail we shall discuss a simpler model which will allow us to develop ideas and techniques which will be needed to deal with the Williamson model.

7.2 A simple managerial model

Suppose we argue that, as well as being interested in the profits gained by their companies, managers are also interested in their own emoluments or 'perks' such as large company cars, expensive paintings in their offices and so forth. It might perhaps be argued that this is particularly likely in the case of modern

[1]See, for example, M. Shubik, Objective functions and models of corporate organisations, *Quarterly Journal of Economics,* August 1961.

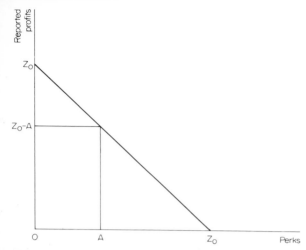

Fig:7.1

firms in which there is a divorce between ownership and control so that increased profits accrue to shareholders rather than to managers while increased perks are enjoyed by the managers themselves. How would a manager who was interested both in profits and in his perks decide on the firm's output and pricing policy? First of all, we can see that the more perks the manager takes the lower the firm's reported profits will be as such perks must be paid for out of the difference between sales revenue and operating costs.[2] This is illustrated by the line in Fig. 7.1. The line has a slope of unity, showing that each pound which is spent on perks reduces reported profits by one pound. Hence if no perks are taken reported profits may be Z_o, if no profits are reported then perks to the value Z_0 may be taken, while if perks to the value A are taken reported profits will be Z_0-A.

The manager can choose the combination of perks and reported profits which he feels is best. This choice process is sometimes represented by a device known as an *indifference curve*. We begin by imagining any combination of profits and perks. This

[2]We assume that there is no relationship between perks and sales revenue or operating costs. It is possible that more perks might increase the manager's effectiveness and this might in turn enable him to find ways of increasing sales revenue or reducing costs.

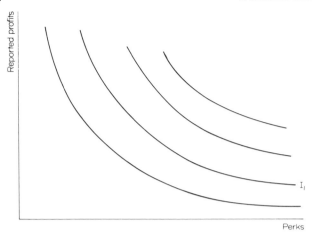

Fig:7.2

will give a certain satisfaction to the manager. We then draw a curve similar to a contour line in a geographic map which connects all other combinations which give equal satisfaction or *utility*. One such curve is I_1 in Fig. 7.2. The curve will be downward sloping if the manager likes both profits and perks, for if one of the two is reduced the other must be increased before he can obtain the same satisfaction. It will be curved if a relative scarcity of either profits or perks increases the valuation which the manager places on them. For example, if he has large profits and few perks he may be prepared to sacrifice a certain amount of profit to gain some perks. However, if he has small profits and many perks he may be equally satisfied but he would now be prepared to give up only a small amount of profits for the same gain in perks. The position of the curve I_1 is determined by the initial combination of profit and perks which we selected. Had we chosen an initial combination having higher profits and more perks the manager would have gained more satisfaction. Hence it is possible to imagine a whole series of indifference curves such as those in Fig. 7.2. All points on one curve give equal satisfaction but all points on a higher curve give more satisfaction than those on a lower one.[3]

[3]A discussion of the theory of indifference curves can be found in any of the microeconomics textbooks listed at the end of Chapter 2.

Combining Figs 7.1 and 7.2 shows the combination of reported profits and perks which the manager will choose. In order to attain the highest level of satisfaction the manager will choose from all the possible combinations of profits and perks that combination which lies on the highest indifference curve. This will occur when the profits/perks line of Fig. 7.1 is as far from the origin as possible and when the line is tangential to an indifference curve. This is illustrated in Fig. 7.3. The figure shows a number of interesting features. First, the profits/perks line will lie as far as possible from the origin when the firm is maximising the difference

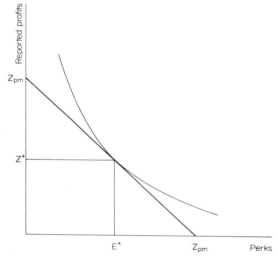

Fig:7.3

between sales revenue and operating costs. Hence if no perks were taken, the firm's reported profits would be equal to those obtained by a profit maximising firm of the kind discussed in Chapter 3. For this reason the vertical intercept of the profits/perks line is labelled Z_{pm}. However, given the manager's indifference curve he will not report profits of Z_{pm} but will instead choose to take some perks, shown by E^* (for emoluments) and to report lower profits, shown by Z^*.

Hence, we can conclude that the manager will choose the same output and price combination as the simple profit maximiser

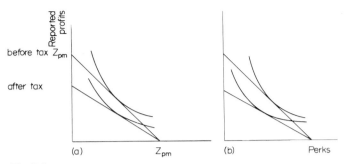

Fig:7.4

but that his costs will be higher and hence his reported profits will be lower because of the perks he takes.

As the output and price combination chosen is the same as that of the simple profit maximiser, it follows that the changes in price and output which the manager will make in response to changes in the firm's situation will in general be the same as those indicated in Table 3.1 at the end of Chapter 3. However, the manager has more freedom of choice because he can vary the proportion of profits and perks which he takes. For example, suppose reported profits become subject to tax but perks are tax-deductible. Suppose further that the shareholder and the manager obtain satisfaction from after-tax rather than pre-tax profits. The introduction of the tax swings the line in Fig. 7.1 anticlockwise, as shown in Fig. 7.4(a). This may well encourage the manager to take more perks and hence to reduce his pre-tax reported profits in order to reduce his tax liability. Although this course of action may seem likely, other courses are possible. For example, the introduction of the tax reduces the after-tax profits of the firm. If the indifference curves are such that small reductions in profits cause large reductions in satisfaction the manager may minimise the fall in profits by giving up many perks. This will be reflected in the shape of the indifference curves, as shown in Fig. 7.4(b).

7.3 The Williamson model

Williamson elaborates on the general idea that managers of modern firms do not have a single objective. He argues that the separation between ownership and control allows managers considerable freedom to follow their own objectives independently of those of the shareholders as long as they meet minimum profit and dividend levels and maintain an adequate rate of growth of the firm over time. He argues further that managers obtain satisfaction from their own salaries and bonuses, from the number and quality of non-production staff who report to them, from the extent to which they are able to influence the future development of the firm by their control over investment expenditure, and from the amount of perks which they enjoy.

A treatment of the full model is beyond the scope of this book, but if we make some simplifying assumptions we can illustrate the core of Williamson's theory. In particular, we shall assume

(i) that managers' salaries depend on after-tax reported profits,

(ii) that the number and quality of its staff depends on the firm's expenditure on staff,

but we shall ignore the satisfaction which managers may derive from the control of investment. These simplifications mean that we can treat managerial satisfaction as an increasing function of reported profits, expenditure on staff, and perks. If expenditure on staff could be treated simply as a perk it would be simple to analyse managers' behaviour by following the same lines of reasoning as those laid out in Section 7.2. However, Williamson argues that expenditure on staff cannot be so treated as the greater the number and quality of its staff the further to the right the firm's demand curve and the greater the sales revenue associated with each level of output. Hence, expenditure on staff may be treated in the same formal way as expenditure on advertising in Section 4.3, and as in the Baumol model in Chapter 6.

We shall first consider the firm's decisions about reported profits and expenditure on staff and for the moment assume that managers receive no perks. Figure 4.8 can be used to illustrate the effects of increased expenditure on staff on the firm's sales revenue and cost curves. As expenditure on staff increases so costs increase as shown by the curves C_1, C_2 and C_3, but so does sales revenue, as shown by the curves R_1, R_2 and R_3. If we assume, as in the case of advertising, that equal additions to cost will eventually lead to declining additions to revenue we can draw the profit curves associated with Fig. 4.8. When expenditure on staff is equal to S_1 the relationship between costs and output is shown by C_1 and that

between revenue and output by R_1. Taking the difference between
revenue and cost allows us to plot the curve labelled S_1 in Fig. 7.5
showing the relationship between profits and output when expenditure on staff is equal to S_1. Changes in the expenditure on staff
give rise to the series of curves in Fig. 7.5 (S_0, S_1, S_2, S_3, S_4).

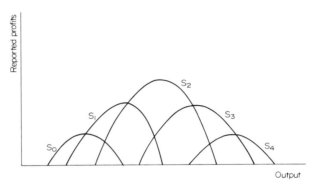

Fig:7.5

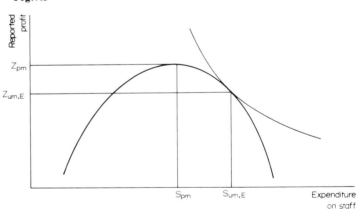

Fig:7.6

The curves in Fig. 7.5 show that for each level of expenditure
on staff there is a maximum possible profit which can be attained
by an appropriate choice of output. We can, therefore, draw a
further curve which shows the relationship between the maximum
possible profit and the level of expenditure on staff. This curve is

shown in Fig. 7.6. It indicates that, at first, expenditure on staff and maximum possible profits move together but that eventually expenditure on staff can be increased only at the expense of profits.

If we draw an indifference curve to show how the manager's satisfaction depends on profit and expenditure on staff we see that he will maximise his satisfaction by choosing a combination such as $Z_{um,E}$ and $S_{um,E}$ (um denotes utility maximising quantities and the other subscript, E, denotes that the level of emoluments is fixed). Comparison between this combination and the profit maximising combination (Z_{pm} and S_{pm}) shows that the satisfaction maximising manager chooses a higher level of expenditure than the profit maximising manager, even though this reduces his reported profit. The profit maximising manager will not increase his expenditure on staff beyond the point where the resulting increase in sales revenue is only just equal to the increase in expenditure, while the satisfaction maximising manager will be prepared to increase his expenditure on staff beyond this point as long as the increase in satisfaction gained by having a more expensive staff exceeds the decrease in satisfaction caused by the consequent reduction in profits.

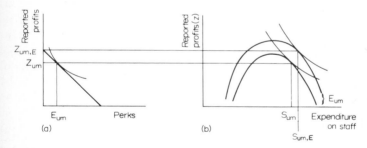

Fig:7.7

Suppose we now introduce a variable level of perks into the model. To do this we need to consider figures such as 7.3 and 7.6 together. This is shown in Fig. 7.7. Part (a) is similar to Fig. 7.3 except that the vertical intercept now shows $Z_{um,E}$, the level of profits resulting from the level of expenditure on staff which maximises satisfaction when perks are zero, rather than maximum possible profits. As we discussed in Section 7.2, the manager will normally choose some perks thus further reducing the level of reported profits below the maximum possible. Figure 7.7(b) shows that the decision to take some perks shifts the profit/staff expenditure curve downwards by an amount equal to the cost of the perks. As we have drawn the diagram this shift causes managers to reduce their expenditure on staff somewhat but, depending on the shapes of the indifference curves, this need not always be the case.

By comparing E_{um}, S_{um} and Z_{um} with their profit maximising values we can conclude that if managers maximise satisfaction rather than profits:

   (i)   they will take more perks,
   (ii)   they will spend more on staff,
   (iii) reported profits will be lower,
   (iv)   reported profits plus cost of perks will be lower,
   (v)   output will be greater,
   (vi)   selling price will be higher.

7.4 Changes in the firm's situation

We may now examine the firm's likely reaction to various changes in its situation. As it can influence the demand for its product, it will be operating in a price searcher's market. Our analysis of firms' responses to change will be again based on the simple assumption of a straight-line, downward sloping demand curve. The reader should by now be in a position to work out the different results that might emerge if we considered any of the special forms of demand curves.

(i) An outward shift in one firm's demand curve (market demand unchanged)

The effects of a shift away from the origin on the firm's demand curve can be seen by referring back to Fig. 4.8. If combinations such as C_1, R_1 and C_2, R_2 represent its cost and revenue situation before the shift, combinations such as C_1, R_2 and C_2, R_3 will represent its situation after the shift. Hence each of the profit curves of the kind shown in Fig. 7.5 will shift outwards so that the maximum possible profit increases and also the range of output over which profits may be made widens. Hence the reported

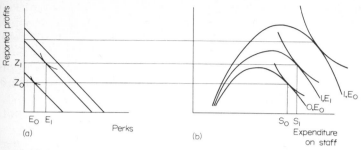

Fig:7.8

profit/staff expenditure curve of the kind shown in Fig. 7.6 will shift in a similar way. The effects of the outward shift in the firm's demand curve are summarised in Fig. 7.8.[4] The levels chosen by the firm before the shift in its demand curve are given the subscript 0 and those after the shift 1. If the firm's manager chose to leave the amount of perks unchanged, his profits/staff expenditure curve would shift out, as shown by the comparison between the lower curve, labelled $0,E_0$, and the upper curve, labelled $1,E_0$. However, the increased profit opportunity shifts the profit/perks line with the result that the firm's manager would choose to increase his perks, thus shifting the profits/staff expenditure curve down a little. Hence we can conclude that expenditure on staff will be increased from S_0 to S_1 and perks will be increased from E_0 to E_1. The firm's price, output and reported profits will also be increased.

Unfortunately, unlike many of the earlier models which we discussed, the Williamson model does not allow us to state any results without qualification. The reason for this is that, quite apart from any doubts about the way in which the firm's demand curve is shifted by changes in expenditure on staff, the results depend on the manager's relative evaluations of the various items determining his satisfaction, and different evaluations will lead to different responses. This may be seen by drawing indifference curves of different shapes and verifying that the preferred tangency points vary accordingly. Nevertheless, if reported profits, expenditure on staff and perks each increase the manager's

[4]Following the same kind of argument as that laid out in Section 4.3 and treating expenditure on staff in the same way as advertising. In this section we assume that increased expenditure shifts the demand curve as shown in Fig. 4.6(a) and (c) and not as in Fig. 4.6(b).

satisfaction, it is unlikely that he will fail to increase each of them i
the opportunity arises and so our conclusion is probably the mos
reasonable. The greater the change in the firm's demand and henc
the greater the amount by which each item contributing to th
manager's satisfaction can be increased, the more likely it is tha
his relative evaluation of each will alter and the more likely i
that he will increase one or two items and reduce the others.[5]

(ii) A fall in the number of firms in the market

The firms which remain in the market will find their deman
curves shifting away from the origin. They will therefore react i
the same way as the firm discussed in (i)

(iii) An increase in market demand

Each firm will find itself in the situation of the firm discusse
in (i) and will react accordingly.

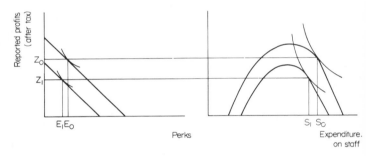

Fig:7.9

(iv) An increase in lump sum taxation

An increase in lump sum taxation shifts the profits/sta
expenditure curve downwards and the profits/perks line toward
the origin, as shown in Fig. 7.9. Given the manager's indifferenc
curves shown in the figure, this will induce the manager to reduc
his expenditure on staff and his perks as well as accepting lowe
reported profits. As argued in Section 4.3, a lower level c
expenditure on staff (like advertising) will shift the firm's sale
revenue curve and this will encourage the firm to reduce its outpu
and lower its price. Again there can be no generality about thes

[5]This is discussed in many microeconomics textbooks, often while dealin
with the choice between taking leisure and working to gain income.

esults. For example, the manager's salary depends on his reported profits and if his satisfaction falls rapidly as his salary falls he may ecide to maintain the same level of reported profits by giving up ome of his perks.

If all firms are subject to the same increase in taxation then hey will face a combination of the situation shown in Fig. 7.9 and hat shown in Fig. 7.8. If some firms leave the market then those vhich remain will experience a further shift in their demand urves.

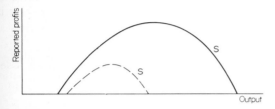

Fig:7.10

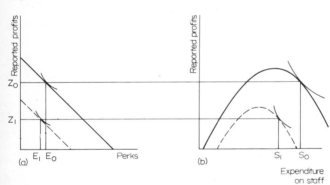

Fig:7.11

(v) An increase in output taxation

The effects of an increase in output taxation are shown in Figs 7.10 and 7.11. Figure 7.10 shows one of the curves of the kind drawn in Fig. 7.5. Each such curve shows how reported profit varies with output as the level of expenditure on staff is held constant. The situation before the rise in taxation is shown by the unbroken line and that after the rise by the broken line. Because the amount of tax varies with output, the reduction in profits which results from the tax will be greater the greater the output which is being produced. It can be seen that, given the level of expenditure on staff, both the maximum possible amount of profit and also the output which produces this amount are reduced. Because the amount of tax increases with output it will be impossible to earn profits at all at the upper ranges of output and staff expenditure so that the profits/staff expenditure curve shifts as indicated in Fig. 7.11(b). This in turn shifts the profits/perks line as indicated in Fig. 7.11(a). With the indifference curves shown, the manager will be induced to reduce output, expenditure on staff, perks and reported profits. The reduction in output will tend to raise price while the reduction in expenditure on staff will tend to lower it.

If all firms are subject to the same increase in taxation then they will face a combination of the situation shown in Fig. 7.11 and that shown in Fig. 7.8.

(vi) An increase in variable costs

If the costs of variable inputs increase then the size of the increase in costs will be greater the greater the output which is being produced. Hence the reduction in profits will be greater the greater the output and the situation is similar to that discussed in (v) and the same conclusions follow.

(vii) An increase in fixed costs

If the firm continues to use the same fixed inputs then the situation will be similar to that of an increase in lump sum taxation discussed in (iv). If the change in costs induces the firm to vary its inputs the situation will be similar to that discussed in Section (iv).

(viii) An increase in profits taxation

The effects on the firm of an increase in the rate of profits taxation are shown in Fig. 7.12. The unbroken lines repeat those of Fig. 7.7 and show the situation before the imposition of the tax. The broken lines show the effects of the tax. Starting with part (b) of the figure we see that the tax shifts the profits/staff expenditure curve downwards by an amount proportional to the original height of the curve. The manager's reactions depend on the shape of his indifference curves. As we have drawn them they indicate that if he was unable to alter his perks from E_0 he would choose to

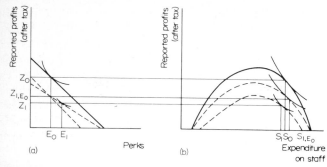

Fig:7.12

increase his expenditure on staff. This seems a reasonable reaction as such expenditure is free of tax. Part (a) of the figure shows that if the manager's perks remained at E_0 his reported profits would be Z_{1,E_0}. If perks and reported profits were both subject to the same rate of tax, the profit/perks line would simply shift to the left as shown by the broken line parallel to the unbroken line and passing through the point E_0, Z_{1,E_0}. However, perks are not subject to tax so that if the manager takes an extra pound's worth of perks his (after tax) reported profits fall by less than one pound (i.e. £1 – tax).

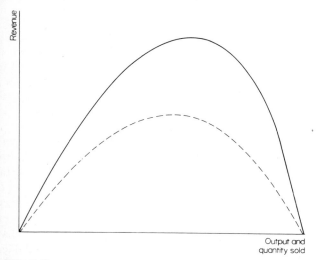

Fig:7.13

Hence he is free to choose any combination on the other broker line passing through the point E_0, Z_{1,E_0}. Given the indifference curves which we have drawn he chooses to increase his perks to E_1 Again, the tax free nature of perks makes this a reasonable assumption. This further reduces the profits/staff expenditure curve drawn in Fig. 7.12(b) and the manager chooses an expenditure equal to S_1. Hence the increase in profits taxation induces the manager to take more perks, to reduce his expenditure on staff, to reduce his output, to lower his price and to accept a lower level of reported profits.

If all firms face the same tax then they will face a combination of the situation shown in Fig. 7.12 and that shown in Fig. 7.8.

Table 7.1
Objective: managerial utility maximisation

Change in firm's situation	Firm's response:				
	Output	Price	Reported profits	Perks	Staff expenditure
(i), (ii), (iii) Expansion in demand curve	+	+	+	+	+
(iv) Increase in lump sum tax	−	−	−	−	−
(v) Increase in output tax	−	+	−	−	−
(vi) Increase in variable costs	−	+	−	−	−
(vii) Increase in fixed costs	−	+	−	−	−
(viii) Increase in profits tax	−	−	−	−	−
(ix) Increase in sales tax	−	+	−	−	−

(ix) An increase in sales taxation

The effects of a tax on the firm's sales revenue may be seen by referring back to Fig. 4.8. If the revenue curves in this figure represent pre-tax revenues associated with particular expenditures on staff, the post-tax curves lie below them as indicated in Fig. 7.13. This means that no after-tax profits can be gained if the firm chooses very high levels of expenditure on staff (for example, the post-tax revenue curve associated with a high revenue curve such as R_3 in Fig. 4.8 will lie below the cost curve C_3 so that the profits/staff expenditure curve will shift as shown in Fig. 7.11. Hence the firm will react in the way discussed in (v).

If all firms are subject to the same increase in tax they will face a combination of the situation shown in Fig. 7.11 and that shown in Fig. 7.8.

7.5 Summary

Our conclusions are again summarised in tabular form (Table 7.1). The reader should bear in mind that the conclusion depends on the shape of the manager's indifference curve and that they can only be taken as a guide to what seems reasonable.

Suggestions for further reading

O.E. Williamson, *The Economics of Discretionary Behaviour,* Markham 1967.
A.A. Alchian, The basis for some recent advances in the theory of the firm, *Journal of Industrial Economics,* November 1965.
M. Silver, Managerial discretion and profit maximizing behaviour, *Journal of Industrial Economics,* April 1967.
O.E. Williamson, Managerial discretion and business behaviour, *American Economic Review,* December 1963.
G.K. Yarrow, Managerial utility maximization under uncertainty, *Economica,* May 1973.

8
The dynamics of business behaviour [1]

8.1 Introduction

In earlier chapters we have had the opportunity to examine
the various possible patterns of firms' behaviour by using a basic
model and modifying it to deal with each of the possible objectives
which a firm might pursue. We have seen the equilibrium values of
the variables entering into the firm's choice set and also the likely
changes in these values which result from changes in the firm's
situation.

The framework adopted so far has been abstract in some
respects. In particular, the reader will have noticed that time has
not really been introduced into the model. The implicit
understanding has been that the equilibrium values of the
variables, once attained, maintain themselves from one period to
the next. This type of model is usually referred to as *static*. The
term 'static' does not necessarily imply criticism of the model
which, after all, has enabled us to derive many predictions about a
wide variety of situations. A static model is, however, limited when
it comes to analysing growth phenomena. Here it is important to
have a clear time dimension. The growth of the firm, like the
growth of the economy, is one of the most important features of
economic life. We must, therefore, extend the framework to deal
explicitly with those decisions which concern the growth of the
firm over time. The type of model which we shall use is often
referred to as *dynamic*. Again it must be noted that the term does

[1]This chapter was written by Nic Zafiris, Senior Lecturer in Economics,
Middlesex Polytechnic.

not imply superiority of dynamic models over static ones in general. Many static models are perfectly adequate to capture the main features of the phenomena which they represent and, if that is the case, there may be little or nothing to be gained from the introduction of additional complications. Yet it cannot be denied that dynamic models are more general. Typically, they cover all the ground covered by static ones in the form of special cases. For that reason many economists prefer to work almost exclusively with dynamic models.

It turns out that many concepts used in static models can readily be translated into dynamic terms. Take the concept of profit, for example. In static theory it is a timeless magnitude which the firm maximises in the typical 'period'. But more realistically we can visualise the firm maximising its profits *over time*. The magnitude with which we are now concerned is the whole 'stream' of profits which are expected to accrue in the future. The firm now maximises, broadly speaking, the sum of these expected future profits. Generally, it is these future profits that determine the capital value of the owners' interest in the firm, so the counterpart of our profit maximisation model in elementary dynamic theory is a model in which the firm maximises its capital value.

The same idea is often expressed in somewhat vaguer terms when it is claimed that the firm maximises its long-run rather than its short-run profits. But, notwithstanding the definitional problems which this formulation raises, it still recognises that there must be a conflict between profits now and profits later and that it is important to consider the total future profile of profits and not concentrate myopically on the current period alone.

8.2 Evaluating streams over time

We must now make more precise the idea of capital value. We have already indicated that it depends on the firm's future profits. These may be received by the owners in the period in which they occur or they may be reinvested to increase profits in later periods. In either case it is the actual receipts which are of significance in the determination of the capital value of the owners' interest. Reinvested profits are only of significance in so far as they result in ultimate receipts by the owners.[2] The sum of future receipts which can be expected by the owners—or the prospective buyers of the firm or of shares in the case of a company—is thus the capital value of the owners' interest. It is the value of the proprietor's holding in a small business or the value of the ordinary shares in a company.

However, the sum of future receipts which gives us the capital value is not a simple one. The present owners of the firm, as well as its prospective buyers, are likely to attach more weight to cash now than to cash which they expect to receive in the future. This phenomenon is referred to, rather loosely, as *time preference* or *positive time preference* to indicate that present receipts are preferred over future receipts. It may be due to one or more of a number of reasons which have been put forward by economists. It may, for example, be due to the individual's short-sightedness and concern with his present needs at the expense of his future ones, or to uncertainty about his survival which obviously must increase with the remoteness of the expected receipts. Furthermore, he may consider the uncertainty surrounding the receipts to increase with time although that may not necessarily be true. But there is also the simple fact that money received now can be invested and earn a return whereas money received later will forfeit that return in the meantime. Alternatively, if money can only be received later, present expenditures will have to be financed by borrowing, on which interest is payable. Last but not least, it will be recognised that expectations of inflation may increase the relative desirability of present receipts. Inflationary expectations will generally induce investors to demand a higher return on their investments than expectations of constant prices and this will exert an upward pressure on interest rates. The adjustment is often partial but it can generally be expected that the market rate of interest will include an allowance for inflation. It is ultimately the fact that borrowing is costly and that lending yields a return which induces the investor to attach less weight to future receipts than to present ones. For the same reason the weight decreases with the remoteness in time of the receipts concerned.

[2]We assume here that the market demand curve for the firm's product is shifting away from the origin over time so that profits can be gained by expanding the firm.

How may an investor evaluate any opportunities presented to him? One way is to compare the opportunity with the best alternatives that are open to him. Suppose the rate of interest is i. Then, if he lends a sum of money S, he can receive a sum $S(1+i)$ next year, or a sum $S(1+i)^2$ after two years, or a sum $S(1+i)^3$ after three years and, in general, a sum $S(1+i)^n$ after n years.[3] If we now think of the amount that the man must lend now in order to receive a certain amount in the future then we can see that to receive an amount M in n years' time, the man must lend $M/(1+i)^n$ now[4] Suppose the man is presented with the opportunity to receive a sum D in n years' time, for a certain price. If this price is less than $D/(1+i)^n$ then the man makes more on the deal than he could make by lending his money at a rate of interest i; but if the price is more than $D/(1+i)^n$ the man would do better to lend his money. Hence one way to evaluate a potential investment is to compare its price with the amount of money which must be lent now to give a return equal to that offered by the investment. This amount of money is known as the *present value* of the investment. We have seen already that the present value of a sum D in n years' time is $D/(1+i)^n$. This can be generalised to show that the present value of a stream of returns D_t covering a number of years up to year n is

$$V = \frac{D_1}{(1+i)} + \frac{D_2}{(1+i)^2} + \frac{D_3}{(1+i)^3} + \frac{D_4}{(1+i)^4} + \frac{D_5}{(1+i)^5} + \cdots + \frac{D_n}{(1+i)^n} \qquad (8.1)$$

where V denotes present value. The greater the difference between V and the price which must be paid for the investment opportunity the better the opportunity relative to that afforded by lending one's money at a rate of interest i.[5]

The valuation of a business from the point of view of its owners or any potential investors in it is another application of the simple technique of investment appraisal. If D_t denotes the receipts anticipated in period t by the investors in the firm and i is the appropriate rate of interest, equation (8.1) is the expression which will yield the present value of the firm.

[3] The reader who is unfamiliar with algebra should verify the formula by calculating the value of £100 invested at 10% ($i = 0.1$).

[4] As in n years' time $M/(1+i)^n$ will produce $[M/(1+i)^n](1+i)^n = M$.

[5] The reader should verify that the same remark is true if we substitute borrowing for lending, as a sum S borrowed now will have to be paid back as $S(1+i)^n$ in n years' time.

In many models the stream of future receipts can usefully be thought of as an infinite one. The choice really depends on our views about the investor's 'horizon', that is the time period over which he is willing to make guesses about the likely magnitude of the expected receipts. But in our case the calculation of present value, sometimes known as *discounting,* ensures that the present value of very remote receipts is an unimportant part of the sum. So postulating an infinite horizon may not be a bad approximation to a reasonably long horizon in reality.

A word is in order at this point about the nature of calculations such as that in equation (8.1). First, we can regard it as a model of rational behaviour: a formula to use when assessing the value of a prospective investment. The value, once calculated, can be compared with the cost of the investment or with the value of other investments which may be contemplated. A decision on whether the investment is worthwhile can then be made. We can say that this conception of the operation is a normative one. The formula is an instrument for certain types of economic decisions. However, we are taking a further step here. As elsewhere in the field of economics, we are postulating rational action to explain behaviour. We try, that is, to capture investors' real-world behaviour through a model which postulates that they act rationally and use the method of discounting shown in equation (8.1) to appraise their investments. We are now back in the field of positive economics as a behavioural science rather than as a set of techniques for optimal calculation. The reader is reminded that for the validation of such a model it is not necessary to observe investors actually performing the calculations postulated. All that is required is that the predictions derived from the model be capable of verification. It will then be 'as if' investors actually behaved in the way the model describes.

A moment's reflection will show that the step from a normative to a positive model in the present context is not entirely unwarranted, for it is reasonable to suppose that the investor, acting in his own interest, will in fact follow, however crudely, an approach similar to the one postulated. Indeed, the number of successful new books and pamphlets describing discounting techniques indicates that many people attempt to follow this approach. Application of the formula in equation (8.1) will yield

he present value of an income stream which can then be compared
o the cost of the titles to that stream (say the ownership of a small
business or of a share in a large company). If the present value of
he receipts exceeds the cost of purchasing the titles to them the
investment will be undertaken.

This is the basic process from the point of view of the
individual investor, but other investors will also go through
similar processes. Although they will not all agree about the
expected income streams from particular investments their views
will probably converge to an overall expectation about each one.
There will also be a common perception of alternative
opportunities and a common view of the correct rate of interest to
use in the discounting process. It can thus be expected that a
generally agreed view of each investment will be established by the
market. That will, in turn, determine the market price of the titles
to the investment, in this case the market values of the businesses
concerned.

The market values of businesses need not be stable. At any
moment there are likely to be investors whose valuation of a
business will exceed that of the market and who will therefore seek
to acquire titles of ownership in it. There will also be those who
want to sell their interests in the same business because their view
of its future earnings is less optimistic than those generally held.
Market values will not be disturbed by such transactions unless an
imbalance appears in the relative desires to buy and sell. But such
an imbalance would indicate a shift in the general expectation of
the prospects of a business and would eventually be translated into
a higher or lower market value which will appear realistic in the
light of revised expectations.

The picture given in the last few paragraphs can conveniently
be summarised in a simple formula. We assume first that there is a
general expectation that the owners' receipts will be maintained at
a constant level D over the infinite future. We make this
assumption mainly for its simplicity, but its economic
interpretation is that the firm operates in a situation of perfect
competition with fixed input and product prices. We also assume
that investors in general require a return of at least i on their
investments. The rate i might perhaps be taken as the rate on long-
term government securities. Given these assumptions, we can sum
the infinite series, derived from equation (8.1):

$$V = \frac{D}{(1+i)} + \frac{D}{(1+i)^2} + \frac{D}{(1+i)^3} + \frac{D}{(1+i)^4} + \cdots + \frac{D}{(1+i)^\infty} \tag{8.2}$$

to give

$$V = \frac{D}{i} \tag{8.3}$$

This model is, of course, very simple but it can be extended without too much difficulty. First it must be recognised that business activity is typically subject to considerable risk. The D are not known in advance and they may even turn out to be negative, involving the investor in a capital loss. He in turn will not be content with returns only just equal to those which he could get on the 'risk free' government security and may evaluate investment at a higher interest than i.[6] Moreover, the degree of risk varies from one type of business to another and hence so will the interest rates used in the discounting process by the market to evaluate the capital values of businesses from their expected earnings.

Secondly, it must be remembered that many investments are undertaken with a view to making capital gains rather than earning a regular income. Such a capital gain may be the result of the growth of the firm's productive capacity and consequently of its annual earnings or it may be due to an upward revision of market expectations concerning the profitability of the business. The latter type of gain is often described as speculative. It depends on the possession of superior judgement or better information on the part of the speculator than that available to the rest of the market.

The present value calculation for a speculator who expects to realise a capital gain at the end of, say, the second year of the investment takes the form

$$V = \frac{D}{(1+i)} + \frac{V_2}{(1+i)^2} \tag{8.4}$$

where V_2 denotes the value realised at the end of year 2. 'Normal' growth of his receipts can also be anticipated by the investor in a present value calculation. Suppose that the owners' receipts are expected to grow at a steady rate g per annum. The market will then attach to the firm a present value of

[6]Even though it might be more rational for him to use the market rate and examine the sensitivity of his calculations to different assumptions about the D.

$$V = \frac{D}{(1+i)} + \frac{D(1+g)}{(1+i)^2} + \frac{D(1+g)^2}{(1+i)^3} + \frac{D(1+g)^3}{(1+i)^4} + \cdots + \frac{D(1+g)^\infty}{(1+i)^\infty} \quad (8.5)$$

hich may be simplified to

$$V = \frac{D}{i-g} \quad\quad\quad (8.6)$$

omparing formula (8.6) with (8.3) we find that the present value ow depends on the growth rate g. It turns out, in fact, that present alue increases at the same rate as the rate of growth of annual eceipts g.[7]

We have now outlined the essential concepts which will help o analyse the firm's behaviour in dynamic terms. Following the 1ethodology of other chapters we shall now postulate different bjective functions for the firm and examine the firm's choice of alues for the variables entering into its choice set and the way in 'hich this choice changes with changes in the firm's ircumstances.

8.3 The dynamics of profit maximisation

Maximisation of the firm's market value is the simplest ossible objective function in the dynamic context. The policies ·ading to maximum present value can easily be derived from quation (8.6). It can be seen by inspection that the maximum alue of V occurs when g is equal to i (in which case the present alue of the firm becomes infinite!). To see the various possibilities 1ore clearly it will help to examine the implications of selecting a articular growth rate. First, it will be seen that any growth will ·quire more capital and this imposes a financial requirement on 1e firm. For simplicity, we shall assume that all the growth of the rm's capital stock is financed entirely from internal sources.[8] Part f the profits will thus have to be retained to be reinvested in the

[7]The reader familiar with calculus can prove this by noting that the elasticity ' V with respect to D is unity as

$$\frac{\partial V}{\partial D} \cdot \frac{D}{V} = \frac{1}{(i-g)} \cdot \frac{D}{D/(i-g)} = 1$$

[8]The assumption is not as restrictive as might appear at first sight. The troduction of new equity capital will lead to a dilution of control and will ·nerally be resisted by the present owners. And more loan capital will be :pensive—if available at all—without 'backing' from new equity. The empirical ·idence shows that internal sources are by far the most significant source of firms 1ance for expansion.

firm. We shall refer to the percentage of profit retained as the *retention rate* and we shall denote it by b. We can now establish a relationship between the chosen growth rate g and the retention rate necessary to achieve this.

It will be recalled that the rate of growth of receipts is also the rate of growth of the firm's capital value.[9] We can therefore write $g = \Delta V/V$. We shall make the simplifying assumption that the acquisition by the firm of new equipment for expansion will increase its market value by the full value of the assets acquired. If so ΔV will also denote the amount of reinvestment required to finance a rate of expansion equal to g. It follows that $\Delta V = gV$. A related simplifying assumption will also be made. This is that the profitability of the firm's future operations will continue as before, that is that a rate of return i will still be produced.[11] Then, if the amount of profits is denoted by Z, we can write $Z = iV$. It now follows that

$$V = bZ$$

or $$gV = biV$$

so that $$g = bi \qquad (8.7)$$

Thus a rate of retention b implies a rate of growth g. Alternatively our target rate of growth requires a retention rate of $b = g/i$. It can be seen in this way that a very close relationship exists between the rate of growth g and the rate of retention b. The firm can select only one or the other but not both.

Inspection of equation (8.6) shows that to maximise V the firm must make g as nearly equal to i as possible, which in turn seems to imply a rate of retention of nearly 1. The result is illustrated in Fig. 8.1.

But under our assumptions, reinvestment must be at the expense of owners' current receipts, i.e. it will lower D in (8.6). The limiting case is, then, not realistic, but it does bring out an important principle, namely that to maximise the firm's present value the maximum ploughback of profits is needed to finance

[9]See footnote 7.

[10]Where Δ denotes 'the change in'.

[11] That i is the rate of profit can also be seen if we solve (8.6) for i. Then $i = D/V + g$. Profits are thus received by the owners of firms in two parts—in the form actual receipts and in the form of capital appreciation of their interest. Also it can be seen that the amount of profits Z, which equals iV, is equal to $D + gV$ or $D + \Delta V$, that is the sum of the owners' receipts plus the reinvestment equals total profits.

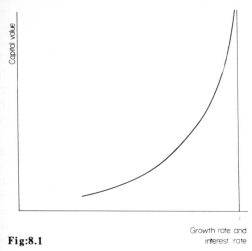

Capital value

Growth rate and
interest rate

Fig:8.1

xpansion.[12] It follows also that maximum profits must be earned
n the present period to make as much finance available as
ossible. Thus the requirements of present value maximisation in
erms of output and price in the present period are the same as the
equirements of simple profit maximisation in the static model!
The required level of output in the current period is the one which
naximises profits and the only difference between the models is
he rate of expansion through time.

The other limiting case, of course, is where all the profit is
aken by the owners and none is retained. In this case the present
alue will consist of the stream of the same maximum profits
epeated every year.

It is, however, unlikely that the owners will decide on either a
ero or a 100% retention policy. A policy of no retention in the case
n hand would imply total absence of investment opportunities for
he firm which would yield a return at least as good as the rate of
rofit currently earned. On the other hand, a policy of 100%
etention would also not find favour with the owners who would
robably be anxious to take out some of their profits. It is true, as

[12]For simplicity we have ignored here the possibility of the rate of return on
ew investment being higher than the current rate of profit. But clearly, so long as
hat is the case it would be in the owners' interest to reinvest profits. Whereas, with
rofitability staying constant at i the rate of investment makes no difference to the
irm's value.

we shall see, that high retention policies are sometimes popular with the management of some companies but they meet with the disapproval of the capital market unless an acceptable minimum of the profits is distributed in dividends at the end of every period. Such disapproval is often expressed through the application of a higher discount rate to the firm's future dividends which reduces the firm's capital value. Thus a 100% ploughback is normally inconsistent with the postulated objective of capital value maximisation.

One further complication must be added for more realism at this point. We must introduce a certain type of cost incurred by the firm as a result of expansion. It arises mainly from the scarcity of management resources, making it difficult to expand the organisation quickly without some loss of efficiency. Expansion costs, such as training new managers, are distinct from ordinary production costs and they constitute an important limitation to the possibilities of growth in the short run. The present value of such expansion costs, like the present value of the owners' receipts can be thought of as a function of the rate of growth g.[13] In symbols

$$V_C = V_C(g) \tag{8.8}$$

This model is superior to the previous one and the rest of the discussion of present value maximisation will be conducted in these terms.

It will now be apparent that the present value which the firm will wish to maximise will not be V_D—the present value of the owners' receipts alone—but the difference between V_D and V_C. The variable which the firm can choose is g, the growth rate.

The decision problem can be illustrated in a simple diagram as shown in Fig. 8.2. We saw earlier that in the absence of expansion costs it was in the interest of the firm to select g as high as possible, but in the revised model what might be called the 'marginal cost of expansion' will soon catch up with the 'marginal returns to expansion'. The optimum will be at the rate g^* in Fig. 8.2 where the present value of the marginal returns of g just equal the marginal costs of g.[14]

[13]We could also write $V_D = V_D(g)$. We shall adopt this notation from now on in place of simply V.

[14]Expressed algebraically, we maximise $V_{net} = V_D(g) - V_C(g)$, or more explicitly $V_{net} = D/(i-g) - V_C(g)$ and the first order condition is $D/(i-g)^2 - V'_C(g) = 0$.

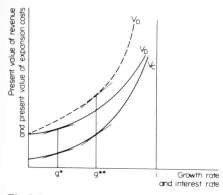

Fig:8.2

We shall now examine the comparative static results, as in arlier chapters.

8.4 Changes in the firm's situation

(i) Changes in demand

If an increase in demand can be expected in the typical period n the future it will cause an increase in the V_D function. V_D will iow be the result of the summation of greater D values in every eriod. That in turn will obviously lead to an increase in the resent value of the firm. To the extent that the increase in demand overs the current period, current output, price and profits will lso rise. The change also implies something about the optimal ate of growth to be selected. As we have seen, the choice of g epends on the relationship between the slopes of the V_D and the V_C curves. Whereas it is clear that the effect of increased demand ill be to shift the V_D curve upwards, the effect on its slope will epend on the exact distribution of the improvement in demand ver the period. On the simplest assumption of a proportional icrease in profits and hence in owners' receipts throughout the iture period the slope of the V_D curve will increase.[15] It can easily e verified from Fig. 8.2 that a higher rate of growth g^{**} will now

---

[15]For example, if the annual increase in profits is, say 20%, V_D at every g will lso increase by 20% because it will equal $1.2D/(1+i) + 1.2D/(1+i)^2 + \cdots + 1.2D/(1+i)^n$ $1.2V_D$. The upward move of the curve will then be more than a parallel shift, nvolving greater absolute increases in V_D at higher values of g.

be selected. The converse effects can be expected from a deterioration in the demand conditions.

(ii) Changes in the rate of interest

We have seen that the market interest rate ultimately governs the rate i which is used to discount future streams. An increase in i will lead to a downward shift in the V_D curve and it will also reduce its slope because the impact of higher i's will be compounded for returns occuring later. A higher i will also shift the V_C curve downwards but here the effect on the slope will probably be negligible as most of the expansion cost will be incurred in the current period. The optimal value of g will therefore move to the left indicating a slowdown of the firm's growth. A fall in the present value of the firm will also take place. A fall in the rate of interest will have opposite effects.

(iii) Changes in taxation

The effects of changes in the different types of taxes on the optimal values of the variables in the current period have already been examined in Chapter 3. We shall add here that the imposition of, or an increase in, taxation will reduce the present value of the firm because taxes reduce profits in future periods in the same way that they reduce profits in the current period.

A lump sum tax will move the V_D curve downwards by its full amount without affecting its slope so that the optimal growth rate will be unchanged. This result holds for a once for all or an annual lump sum tax. In the latter case, of course, the fixed reduction in V_D is the discounted sum of the future annual payments of tax.

A profits tax on the other hand will also reduce the slope of the V_D curve because the tax represents a fixed percentage of V_D at every value of V_D and it will have greater absolute impact on high V_D values. The chosen growth rate will be reduced in this case.

A sales tax levied as a percentage of sales revenue will also reduce both the level and the slope of the V_D curve. We should therefore expect a reduction in the chosen value of g.

An output tax will have very similar effects as the sales tax and will lead to a reduction of g.

(iv) Changes in costs

A permanent change in fixed costs will have the same effect as a change in lump sum taxation while a change in variable cost

would have the same effect as an increase in output taxation.
The results of this analysis are summarised in Table 8.1.

Table 8.1
Objective: present value maximisation (of future return)

Change in firm's situation	Firm's response			
	Current output	Market value	Growth rate	Current product price
Increase in demand	+	+	+	+
Increase in lump sum tax	0	−	0	0
Increase in profits tax	0	−	−	0
Increase in sales tax	−	−	−	+
Increase in output tax	−	−	−	+
Increase in fixed costs	0	−	0	0
Increase in variable costs	−	−	−	+
Increase in interest rates	0	−	−	0

8.5 The dynamics of sales revenue maximisation

For reasons analagous to those given for the corresponding
static case of simple sales revenue maximisation the firm's
managers may be interested in maximising the present value of the
future stream of sales revenue. To show this we can use equations
8.1), (8.5) and (8.6), substituting R for D to indicate sales
revenues.

Growth of sales, like growth of profits, imposes financial
requirements on the firm. On the assumption that growth must be
internally financed, maximum profits in the current period ensure
that the maximum amount of financial resources is available for

expansion of future sales. On the other hand, a greater volume of sales in the current period contributes towards a higher present value of sales, albeit at the expense of some current profits.

A second type of financial requirement has already been alluded to but becomes particularly important in the context of sales revenue maximisation and, indeed, with any objective other than the maximisation of the value of the owners' interest. It stems from the need to provide satisfactory payouts to the owners of the firm. If firms ignore the profit constraint this can be expected to show itself in the capital market. The mechanism envisaged here is that of the takeover. Investors notice that the profits of the firm and consequently its market value, fall short of what the productive potential of the firm's real assets would have led them to expect. They then offer to purchase the owners' interest at a price reflecting the firm's potential earning power rather than its lower earnings profile resulting from the pursuit of the sales maximising objective by the management. The takeover mechanism is often activated when the ratio of the market value of the firm to the total value of its real assets—often called the *valuation ratio*—falls below some critical minimum.

Now managers would be reluctant to be taken over as that would involve loss of autonomy and the risk of being dismissed by the new owners. They could thus be expected to see that the value of the firm does not drop to a level which would expose them to the hazards of a takeover bid.[16] Even apart from this, managers often derive part of their own income from their shareholding in the company and would therefore be interested in a reasonable valuation as owners. In the remainder of this section we shall concentrate on the first type of financial requirement.

The firm which aims to maximise the present value of its sales revenue also has to choose an optimal rate of growth, this time of its sales revenue. A given V_R (for present value of sales) can be achieved by different pairs of values of current sales and growth of future sales, more sales in the current period being at the

[16]The reader will appreciate that the discussion at this stage is almost exclusively concerned with the problems of the company as opposed to the small owner-controlled firm. After all, the owners of small firms have the power to alter retention policies at will whereas the company's shareholders can only influence the managers' policy by selling their shares or by being unusually active at shareholders' meetings.

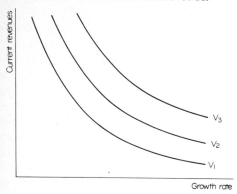

Fig:8.3

xpense of profits and hence at the expense of future growth of ales revenue. The relation between current sales revenue R and he rate of growth of sales revenue (g) can be shown graphically s in Fig. 8.3. Each curve on the graph represents all combinations f R_0 and g which produce the same present value. It is clear that he curves are downward sloping but in general nothing more can e said about their shape.

Figure 8.4 shows the choice of the optimal growth rate. The rofit maximising level of current output, q_{pm}, makes it possible

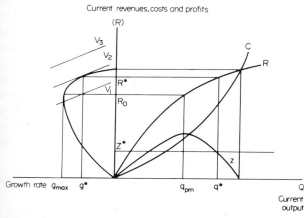

Fig:8.4

to finance the maximum growth of sales revenue but at th cost of achieving only R_0 revenue now. The objective is to achiev the highest present value of sales, that is the highest curve in Fig 8.4 (we have used straight lines to represent the curves fo simplicity). The highest present value that it is possible to reach i V_2 involving a rate of growth g^*, which is less than the maximum possible, and a current sales revenue of R. The level of curren profits which this generates is less than the maximum possible bu it is just enough to finance the rate of growth g^*. That level o profits represents an internally generated constraint on the firm' managers, imposed on them by their objective.

The present value of sales revenue maximisation model is o rather limited interest compared with our earlier model and ou treatment of it has been rather sketchy. Equally, we shall not tr here to offer a full account of its comparative static propertie Some general observations will be made, however.

First, we may note that, whenever an increase in costs o taxation occurs in a situation where a minimum profit constrain exists, the constraint cannot be satisfied after the change unles there is a compensating increase in profits. In the present contex this would require a lower sales revenue in the current period an move in the direction of more profits. This in turn implies a lowe present value of sales revenue with reductions in both component of the present value, i.e. current and future sales revenue.

Second, a permanent increase in market demand will improv the set of opportunities facing the firm and, in particular, wi enable it to earn higher sales revenue and profits. It will now b feasible to finance a rate of growth of sales revenue higher than i the previous situation. The effect of larger current sales and faste growing sales is obviously to increase the present value of sales.

Finally, a rise in the rate of interest will reduce the presen value of future sales and increase the relative desirability of curren sales. The new maximum present value of sales revenue wi involve more current and hence less future sales revenue and lower rate of growth of sales revenue.

8.6 The dynamics of managerial utility maximisation

Our summary of dynamic extensions of the various models o

he firm would not be complete without some discussion of the
managerial utility model. The ideas in this field are still in a state of
flux and a full account of the results obtained from the various
alternative models would take us beyond the scope of this book.
All that we shall do here is to postulate a simple managerial utility
function in the dynamic context and indicate the main results.

The basic utility function takes the form

$$U = U(v,g) \qquad\qquad (8.9)$$

where g is the rate of growth of real assets and v is the valuation
ratio.

In previous models the rate of growth was seen as
instrumental in maximising the present value of variables such as
owners' receipts. Here the rate of growth enters into the utility
function directly as a measure of power and prestige. It can be
expected that it will be company managers who have a utility
function of this sort but we cannot exclude the possibility that the
growth oriented owner might as well. Similarly, the valuation
ratio can also be seen as an indicator of performance but unlike the
growth rate it is of greater significance for owners because of its
more direct impact on their wealth. Managers could therefore
conceivably sacrifice some of the firm's market value in the pursuit
of prestigious—but unprofitable—growth policies. But it is less
easy to imagine similar indulgence on the part of the owners. For
these reasons many writers prefer to think in terms of a minimum
valuation ratio, entering into the manager's optimisation problem
as a constraint,[17] that is a valuation ratio high enough to prevent
takeovers. But, as indicated earlier, to the extent that the
manager's own holdings in the company are significant the firm's
valuation may be of more direct importance to him as well in his
capacity as an owner.

The choice situation is illustrated in Fig. 8.5. The choice set
open to the owner or manager is given by the so-called valuation
curve which depicts the highest valuation ratio which is consistent
with any given growth rate. Its shape indicates that moderate
rates of growth can be expected to raise the firm's valuation ratio
but that after a certain point conflict arises as any further

[17]For managers $U = U(v,g)$ where v indicates the minimum valuation
constraint. The owners' welfare, on the other hand, would simply be $U = U(v)$ and
owners' utility may be a monotonically increasing function of v.

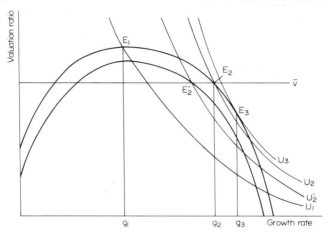

Fig:8.5

growth—which devotes more assets to unprofitable investment—must be at the expense of some of the firm's potential capital value. The indifference curves in the figure measure managerial utility as defined in equation (8.9). On the other hand the owners' welfare can be considered for simplicity to be measured by the valuation ratio itself. Then E_1, the maximum point on the valuation curve, will give the optimum pair of values from the owners' point of view. This, however, represents a welfare level of only U_1 for the managers. They would be inclined to choose E_3 producing a utility of U_3 and have a higher growth rate and a lower valuation ratio than the owners. But the capital market may impose a restriction on the managers to produce a valuation ratio of $\bar{v}$, in which case they will choose E_2, representing the maximum growth rate (g_2) consistent with the valuation constraint. Obviously this means that they can no longer achieve a utility level as high as they could in the absence of the constraint and they now have to be content with utility level U_2.

Turning now to the effects of changes in the firm's situation, we can see that, as in the other models, higher costs will reduce the firm's profits. This in turn will reduce the receipts which the owners can ultimately expect, whatever the firm's retention policy, and this will reduce the capital value of the firm. It will now not be possible to meet any minimum valuation requirement which could just be met previously unless financial resources which were previously allocated to achieve an optimal growth rate are diverted to maintain the minimum payout expectations of the owners. But it will now only be possible to reach a lower growth rate within the minimum valuation constraint.

In terms of Fig. 8.5 the valuation curve shifts downwards indicating the inferior choice set open to the firm. The new equilibrium E_2 in the case of the minimum valuation constraint will involve a lower growth rate. Similar results hold for increases in taxes. The precise way in which the curve moves depends on the type of cost increase or tax increase. Lower costs or lower taxes will have symmetrically opposite effects.

It is worth noting that cost and tax changes applying all across industry will have less effect than discriminatory taxes against particular firms, or isolated cost increases affecting only a particular group of firms, because a general deterioration of profitability in industry will lead investors to revise their expectations downwards and will prevent them from taking their funds elsewhere if their requirements are not met by their present firm.

Improved conditions, on the other hand, will give managers greater freedom to pursue discretionary policies within, say, a minimum valuation constraint. A higher rate of growth will be selected and possibly a higher valuation ratio as well. However, a general rise in interest rates will reduce the present value of the firm and make it impossible for it to continue to meet the minimum valuation constraint while maintaining the same growth rate. Taking the simplest case, where the valuation ratio is only a constraint for management, a lower growth rate will be needed to reduce the sacrifice of profits and to enable management once again to meet the minimum aspirations of the owners of the firm.

Suggestions for further reading

R. Marris, *The Economic Theory of 'Managerial' Capitalism*, Macmillan 1964.
W.J. Baumol, On the theory of expansion of the firm, *American Economic Review*, Dec. 1962.
J.H. Williamson, Profit, growth and sales maximisation, *Economica*, Feb. 1966.
E. Penrose, *The Theory of the Growth of the Firm*, Blackwell 1959.
R. Marris and A. Woods (eds), *The Corporate Economy*, Macmillan 1971.
J.K. Galbraith, *The New Industrial State*, Penguin 1969.
M. Gordon, *The Investment, Financing and Valuation of the Corporation*, Irwin 1962.

9
Tests and conclusions

9.1 Introduction

We can now turn to the problem of testing the many
hypotheses that have been considered and the many assertions
that have been made throughout the book.

9.2 Interviews and questionnaires

It may seem that the best and most obvious way to test is to
make contact with the heads of firms either by interviews or by
questionnaires and ask them what their objectives are. However
even ignoring the practical difficulties involved, this might not be a
fruitful means of testing. The reason is that, as we stated in
Chapter 1, the object of our examination of firms' behaviour is to
allow us to explain the actions which firms have taken in the past
and to predict the actions they will take in the future in response to
changes in their circumstances. Now, even if it was clear that every
firm aimed to maximise its profits, we could not conclude that
firms would take the decisions we predicted because they might
have mistaken views on what to do to maximise profits. For
example, firms may believe that profits can be protected after an
increase in lump sum taxation by increasing their prices even
there is no change in the number of firms in the market. If they
believe this to be so then they will increase their prices even though
this action fails to maximise their profits. This caveat probably
seems unrealistic in the context of the comparative static world
which we have discussed in most of the book, but in the real world

116

which is constantly subject to change it is not so because there is a real possibility that firms might fail to disentangle the effects of one decision from those of the many others which they have to take at the same time. Hence, it might not be clear to them that by increasing their prices in response to a lump sum tax change they have reduced their profits below their potential maximum. A similar problem occurs in the case of large corporations in which a decision may be taken at a high level and become 'watered down' or distorted as it is implemented by the organisation so that what actually occurs may differ from what the original decision makers intended.

Even if this caveat is thought to be unimportant, there are still many practical problems associated with interviews or questionnaires. Some of these are discussed below.

(i) Identifying the corporate objective

In the case of a small firm it may be easy to discover the firm's objectives because a single individual can be identified who takes all the important decisions and who makes the firm's objectives his own. However, in larger firms it may be difficult to discover how the firm's objectives are decided upon. For example, the managing director may claim that his objective is to implement the decisions of his board of directors. It may be possible to discover what the board's objectives are and how they arrive at their decisions, in which case some measure of the corporate objective could be obtained. However, the board's objective is decided collectively by a group of individuals who may each have different objectives so that, unless one individual is always dominant, the board's collective objective may change according to which member manages to persuade the others to accept his views. If this were the case then there would be no systematic objective from which to predict firms' behaviour. The problems of corporate decision making and of the implementation of decisions by the corporation are discussed in specialised works examining firm's behaviour of which that by Cyert and March is a good example.[1]

(ii) Response rate

Most heads of firms are extremely busy, receive many requests for interviews and are responsible for completing a

[1] See, Suggestions for further reading, at the end of this chapter.

number of questionnaires, some of which come from government departments and which they are legally obliged to return. Many would be unable to grant another interview or would be unable to complete another questionnaire so that only partial information would be obtained. This makes the interpretation of replies very difficult, for those which are returned may come only from those heads with time on their hands or those who are exceptionally public spirited and their replies may be unrepresentative of the whole. Unless their degree of unrepresentativeness could be estimated nothing could be inferred about the behaviour of all firms.

(iii) Interpreting replies

The interpretation of the replies obtained would also be difficult as a large number of different replies would be given. Some would be of the kind 'we do our best to provide the customer with what he wants', which is difficult to fit into our theoretical framework because it can be interpreted in a number of ways. In one sense what the customer wants is an excellent product offered free! If this is what the reply means then we would predict the future bankruptcy of the company. In another sense the reply might be taken to mean that the company tries to keep its price as low as possible and hence aims to maximise output subject to a profits constraint. At the other extreme the reply might be taken to mean that the firm examines customers' tastes very thoroughly because by offering attractive goods they can charge high prices and make large profits.

A similar problem arises with multiple objectives. Many firms may reply that they have a number of objectives such as maintaining a certain market share, making a certain return on capital, and so on. It is not clear from the type of reply which objective is overriding. For example, firms may want to maintain a certain market share because they feel that market share is important in its own right or because they know that the maintenance of the share is the best way to make the desired return on capital.

Of course, this is partly a problem of questionnaire design and the good questionnaire will try to extract unambiguous answers. We could, for example, ask the heads of firms which of the following best described their objectives:

(a) profit maximisation
(b) output maximisation
(c) sales revenue maximisation
(d) managerial utility maximisation
(e) present value maximisation.

Even this would probably be insufficiently clear as, for example, many heads might say that they were clearly not profit maximisers as they often refrained from making profits out of a temporary market shortage. However, further questioning might reveal that they did not do so because they felt that such action might antagonise customers and lose them profits in the future. Hence, the decision not to exploit the temporary market shortage is consistent with the objective of profit maximisation over a long period.

A good questionnaire would probably ask firms' heads how they would react to a number of changes in their circumstances, such as those discussed in previous chapters. By examining the answers it should be possible to infer what the heads' objectives really are. If the changes are carefully selected it should also be possible to check the responses for consistency, a further useful piece of information.

(iv) Frankness

It is well known that people do not always answer questions about themselves correctly and there seems to be no reason to suppose that this is not so in the case of firms' heads, particularly if they feel that their answers may give important information to competitors or may be used by the government to decide on restrictive legislation. To the extent that the answers are incorrect, questionnaires would provide no useful information about firms' behaviour.

A well known study is that of R.L. Hall and C.J. Hitch.[2] They interviewed 38 entrepreneurs about their pricing policy. The overwhelming response was that they decided on their selling prices by calculating the variable costs of production, adding on a percentage to cover fixed costs and then adding a further percentage to produce some profits. This might be taken as evidence in favour of some variant of the output maximisation hypothesis, but it is not conclusive. This is because many of the

[2]See, Suggestions for further reading.

firms interviewed were in oligopoly situations and may have faced kinked demand curves. This view is supported by the fact that 17 firms gave their reason for not charging more than full cost as their competitors or potential competitors (including the belief that others would not follow an increase), while 11 gave their reason for not charging less than full cost as 'competitors would follow cuts', and another 9 gave their reason as 'demand is unresponsive to price' which, if based on past experience in which competitors have lowered their prices and hence prevented the firms from increasing their market share, might mean the same. Hence, it is possible that the firms felt that price adjustments were unwise and that the mark-up process merely represented a rule of thumb method of calculating where, in a world of continually changing circumstances, the kink in the demand curve was likely to be found. This interpretation is given some support by Hall and Hitch who comment that full cost pricing to some firms meant working from some traditional or convenient price and adjusting the quality of the article until full cost equalled the given price. Firms acting in this manner would respond to changes in the same way as those deliberately setting out to maximise profits in oligopoly and so the study does not provide enough evidence to reject the profit maximisation hypothesis.

Interviews and questionnaires have also been used to find out about specific aspects of firms' policies. A good example is the study by P.J. Hovell[3] who examined the export marketing policies of 50 companies. Hovell found that many of the companies did not give the maximisation of profits as an objective and many did not decide on price and output by weighing up demand and cost considerations in the way described in the earlier chapters of this book. However, the decisions which they took did not appear to be unduly different from those predicted by the profit maximisation hypothesis.

9.3 Casual empiricism

This approach is perhaps the one most commonly adopted by economists. Broadly speaking, the approach consists of setting out a theory which is consistent with some observed behaviour.

[3]P.J. Hovell, Export pricing policies, *District Bank Review* No 167, September 1968.

Hence, an economist might claim that in oligopoly there is usually a price leader who chooses a price which is then accepted by the others. He might then describe one or more cases where a major producer has altered his price and other producers have followed almost immediately. To give another example, an economist might claim that firms aim to maximise short-run profits and cite Ferranti's pricing policy for the Bloodhound guided missile in the early 1960s. The weakness of this approach is that we can only be sure that the theory is consistent with the examples put forward, and it may be inconsistent with all the other examples which could be found. Now, as we have suggested in Chapter 1, a theory is not very much use as a general theory unless it can be shown to explain the majority of the observations (or possibly the more important observations), and it is not very much use even as a more limited theory dealing with special circumstances unless these circumstances can be explicitly listed so that situations where the theory is likely to be of use can be recognised in advance. The most that casual empiricism can do is to indicate that the theory is compatible with *some* of the observations. If these observations have been selected at random or if there is nothing unusual about them then the theory receives some support, but it is sometimes difficult to avoid the feeling that the observations quoted are the only ones which are consistent with theory!

Perhaps the most convincing example of casual empiricism concerns the growth of management training. It is interesting to note that many of the ideas which originated from economists' development of pure theory were further developed by management accountants and business economists and are now often taught as part of management training. Hence much time is devoted to the practical problems of measuring the costs and revenues associated with one particular product made by a multiproduct and multiplant firm. Again, the techniques of investment appraisal are taught on a wide variety of courses, both for businessmen and for civil servants. Most of these techniques are particularly valuable as means of maximising profits and the widespread interest in them probably indicates that many businessmen are interested in maximising profits and thus provides support for the use of the profit maximising hypothesis.

9.4 Statistical studies

We now turn to the most reputable but also the most difficult way of distinguishing between hypotheses. This is to collect a large volume of evidence about firms and to see whether any of our hypotheses are consistent with the bulk of the evidence. However, as we shall see, there are many problems involved in this process.

One possible method is to collect data on costs and revenue for a number of firms and compare the actual output produced and the actual price charged with those predicted from various hypotheses. What we should ideally like to do is to find how cost and revenue varied with output in each of the years under study so that we could draw a pair of cost and revenue curves for each period. Figure 9.1 shows the type of result which we would obtain. In this figure the subscripts refer to years, so that it shows that there was an expansion in demand between year 0 and year 1 and no change between year 1 and year 2, while costs changed only between year 1 and year 2.

Suppose we had also recorded the actual output in each year as q_0, q_1 and q_2. We could conclude that all the evidence favoured the hypothesis of profit maximisation. However, suppose the

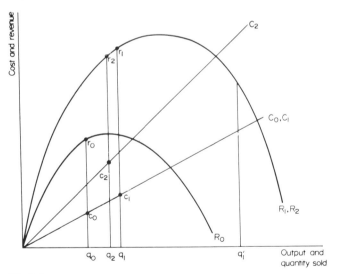

Fig:9.1

actual outputs were q_0 and q_1' and q_2. We might reach any one of a number of conclusions such as:

(i) The firm aimed to maximise profits in years 0 and 2; but aimed to maximise output subject to a profits constraint in year 1.

(ii) The firm aimed to maximise long-run profits, knowing that frequent price changes, particularly those in the face of rising demand, lose customers. Hence, when demand increased, the firm kept its year 0 price and so had a large increase in sales. In year 2 costs rose so much that q_1' could only be produced at a loss and so the firm increased its prices too and reduced its outputs.

(iii) The firm had no clear objective in any year.

Unfortunately, the second type of situation in which the observed outputs do not all support a single hypothesis seems to be the most common.

The data required for this approach are in any case difficult to come by as firms tend to keep them secret in case competitors could profit from them. However, it is sometimes possible to apply the same sort of approach to more limited information. It may, for example, be possible to discover that a multiproduct firm could increase its profits by slightly reducing the output of one product and increasing the output of another. This would indicate that the firm was failing to maximise its profits. It may also be possible to make some deductions from the firm's use of inputs, although we have not considered this aspect of the firm's decision making in the book. For example, if a firm has one plant in an area where labour is cheap and another in an area where labour is expensive then, if substitution between inputs is possible, it would maximise its profits by using a relatively labour intensive production process in the cheap labour area. In a now famous study of firms with plant in both the North and South of the United States, Lester[4] found that they did not use particularly labour intensive methods in the South nor did they make any change in their methods when the differential between North and South narrowed. This suggested that firms did not maximise their profits.

Even if firms are unwilling or unable to provide information

[4]R.Lester, Shortcomings of Marginal Analysis for Wage - Employment Problems. *American Economic Review*, March 1946.

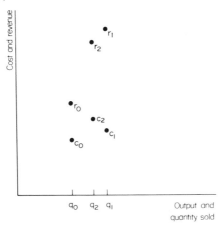

Fig:9.2

showing how costs and revenue varied with output in a number of years, it may still be possible to estimate cost and revenue curves from published data. For example, we may be able to see from the firm's accounts the costs and revenue associated with each year's output. Hence we could obtain the points shown in Fig. 9.2 (which correspond to those shown in Fig. 9.1). Now we cannot draw curves passing close to the points and assume that they represent the firm's cost and revenue curves as the points lie on different curves;[5] but we can examine the changes in wage rates, in customers' incomes, and so on, and try to allow for the effects of such changes on the firm's cost and revenue curves. A common statistical technique for such an analysis is known as *multiple regression analysis*. This process would give us *estimates* of the firm's cost and revenue curves in each year given the actual values of wage rates, customers' incomes, and so on, with which we could carry out the process discussed above.

Unfortunately the use of estimates of the curves rather than the curves themselves raises further problems. This is because, although we can obtain curves which show what we think is the most likely relationship between cost and output and between revenue and output, we cannot be sure that the true relationship is not somewhat different. This is illustrated in Fig. 9.3. The line C

[5]For example, a curve passing close to C_0, C_1 and C_2 would greatly overestimate the slope of the cost curve in any year.

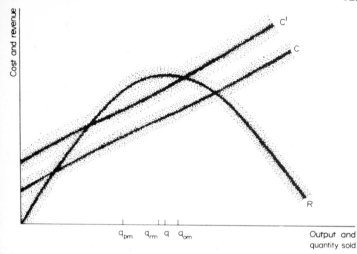

Fig:9.3

shows the cost curve which we think the firm was most likely to have faced in one particular year. The shaded area around C indicates that C is only an estimate of the true curve and that we think that the true curve could well lie anywhere within the shaded region although it is unlikely to lie outside it. A similar reasoning applies to the line R. Now on the horizontal axis we can mark the most likely values for the profit maximising output, q_{pm}, the revenue maximising output, q_{rm}, and the constrained output maximising output, q_{om}. If the actual output was q, then we can argue that the evidence favours the revenue maximisation hypothesis because q is nearer to q_{rm} than to either q_{om} or q_{pm}. However, the presence of the shaded area causes problems because it introduces some uncertainty. For example, if the true value of the revenue curve lay towards the bottom of its shaded area, while the true value of the cost curve lay towards the top of its shaded area then the true value of q_{om} would lie further to the left and could well be nearer to q than q_{rm}, in which case we would argue that the evidence favoured the output maximisation hypothesis. Hence, although the evidence favours the revenue maximisation hypothesis, it doesn't really suggest that the output maximisation hypothesis is wrong.

The higher C relative to R and the wider the areas around them, the less sure we can be about the relative merits of rival hypotheses. For example, if the cost curve is C' then the whole region in which profits can be made lies in a shaded area and hence we have little evidence on which to favour any one hypothesis over any other. Unfortunately, profits are usually small in relation to total costs and total revenue and hence our estimates of C and R are often so close together that the whole of the profits region lies in a shaded area.

These considerations lead us to examine the possibility of using what this book has concentrated on, namely firms' reactions to changing circumstances rather than to one particular circumstance. In this way we would identify a period when a factor such as the rate of taxation on profits had changed and record the changes, if any, which this induced in firms' output and pricing policies. We would then identify another period when a different factor changed and record the effects, if any, which this has on firms' output and pricing policies. After this process had been repeated many times we could compare the actual reactions with those predicted by the various hypotheses and favour the hypothesis whose predictions best accorded with actuality. In this area, as in others, data are scarce and studies have tended to concentrate either on the reactions of a single firm to a number of different changes in its circumstances over a long period[6] or, more commonly, on the reactions of many firms to a single change which affects them all.[7]

Here again there are formidable statistical problems largely caused by the fact that firms' situations are continually changing and by the fact that firms can be expected to take some time to react to changes in their situations. Hence, if there was a sudden increase in wages in one industry which was followed by no further changes then we could observe the decisions made by firms in the industry and any changes in these decisions, however long they took to occur, could be attributed to the wage increase. Similarly, if firms reacted very quickly to changing circumstances we could separate the effects of each of these changes. However, if

[6]See, for example, I.F. Pearce, A study of price policy, *Economica*, May 1956.

[7]See, for example, M. Krzyaniak and R. Musgrave, *The Shifting of Corporate Income Tax*, Johns Hopkins 1963.

ircumstances keep changing and if firms take some time to adjust, hen it is difficult to attribute a particular changed decision to a articular change in circumstances. Of course, this is the usual ituation.

The discussion so far has assumed that it is, in principle, ossible (albeit difficult) to obtain the required statistics and that hey are accurate. A full discussion of these problems would take s too far from our theme, but it is clear that neither assumption nay hold. For example, if we wished to test the Williamson model ve would need figures not just for reported profits but also for the amount of perks which are taken by the managers. It may be mpossible to separate these from the other cost figures which we vould regard as common to all firms, whatever their objectives. Again, many published statistics are prepared from a sample of irms. Before we can use these figures we need to know how accurate they are thought to be, what sort of sample was used, vhether the firms all replied at different times and hence possibly n different circumstances and so on.

9.5 Business behaviour: the statistical evidence

So far in this chapter we have discussed the problems one inevitably encounters in attempts to test the various hypotheses about business behaviour. We shall now summarise and evaluate the relevant available evidence.

Of the existing empirical studies by far the greatest number rely on questionnaire and interview studies; there are relatively few statistical studies. Yet, as we have pointed out, there are inherent weaknesses in the questionnaire and interview method of testing and, as a result, we can find among them little supporting evidence for any of the models of the firm we have been considering. Studies using statistical techniques are more suitable and more reliable for testing alternative theories of the firm. Alas, not only are there relatively few, but not all of them test what we have been focusing attention on in this book, namely firms' reactions to changed circumstances.[8]

[8]Apart from studies testing the comparative static properties of theories of the firm, there are two further groups of empirical study. One other group is concerned with establishing a relationship between market structure, prices and profits. For a survey of these see A. Silberston, Price behaviour of firms, *Economic Journal*,

To test a theory it is essential not just to find evidence which supports a prediction or a number of predictions, but to test those predictions that enable us to discriminate between one theory and any alternative theories that may have been put forward. What seems appropriate, therefore, before evaluating the existing empirical work, is to summarise the various responses we have (with the aid of our different models) predicted; this is done in Table 9.1. What evidence is there to suggest that firms actually behave in the way our models predict? And what evidence can be quoted to suggest that one theory of the firm rather than another yields the more realistic predictions? A number of empirical studies[9] suggest that prices increase with increased demand and, further, demonstrate that prices vary with increased unit costs. More recent evidence[10] also establishes a relationship between cost and price changes. There would, therefore, seem to be little doubt that all our models of the firm appear correctly to explain and predict the relationship between demand and cost changes and pricing policies.[11] But since all models come to the same conclusions, testing firms' responses to demand and cost changes does not enable us to choose between the alternative theories under discussion. There are to our knowledge no studies that seek to establish how firms actually react to a lump sum tax, or increased fixed costs, although it was in dealing with this effect

---

September 1970. A further group attempts to test theories of the firm by looking at the implications of a particular objective function for other problem areas in economics such as income distribution. A good example of this kind of indirect test is J.L. Stein, The predictive accuracy of the marginal productivity theory of wages, *Review of Economic Studies,* June 1958. For a critique of Stein's findings see also G.C. Archibald, Testing marginal productivity theory, *Review of Economic Studies,* February 1959.

[9]See, for example, L.W. Weiss, Business pricing policies and inflation reconsidered, *Journal of Political Economy,* April 1966; T. Hultgren, *Costs, Prices and Profits: their Cyclical Relations,* National Bureau of Economic Research 1965; A.D. Brownlie, Some econometrics of price determination, *Journal of Industrial Economics,* March 1965; O. Eckstein and G. Fromm, The price equation, *American Economic Review,* December 1968.

[10]L. Phlips, Business pricing policies and inflation: some evidence from EEC countries, *Journal of Industrial Economics,* November 1969.

[11]It is worth pointing out in this context that, according to the available evidence, the market structure (or concentration) of any industry does not have any (or only an insignificant) influence on firms' pricing responses. This would justify our simplifications in not distinguishing between different market forms, quite apart from the fact that in our treatment we have been concerned with qualitative predictions, that is the direction, rather than the magnitude, of change.

	Current output	Current price	Sales	Reported profits	Perks	Staff exp.	Market value	Growth rate	Advertising
Increase in demand									
Profit maximisation	+	+	+	+					
Output maximisation	+	+	+	0					
Sales maximisation	+	+	+						+
Utility maximisation	+	+	+	+	+	+			
Present value maximisation*	+	+	+	+			+	+	
Increased fixed costs/lump sum tax									
Profit maximisation	0	0		–					
Output maximisation	–	+	–	0					
Sales maximisation	–	+	–						
Utility maximisation	–	–		–	–	–	–		
Present value maximisation*	0	0		–				0	
Increased variable costs/output tax/sales tax									
Profit maximisation	–	+	–	–					
Output maximisation	–	+		0					
Sales maximisation	–	+	–	–					
Utility maximisation	–	+		–	–	–			
Present value maximisation*	–	+		–			–	–	
Profits tax									
Profit maximisation	0	0		–					
Output maximisation–	–	+	–	0					
Sales maximisation	–	+		–					
Utility maximisation	–	–		–	–	–			
Present value maximisation*§	0	0		0			–	–	

*Present value maximisation of future returns

§Identical predictions would emerge if the present value maximiser was confronted with an increase in the interest rate.

that our alternative hypotheses produced different predictions. There is, however, one study which was designed to subject the sales maximisation hypothesis to an empirical test. In a study based on US data, Hall[12] argued that any positive difference between the actual profits made by firms and the profit constraint (such a difference might come about as a result of a reduced lump sum tax or a reduction in fixed costs) would lead to an increase in sales. The rationale for this argument is of course that a sales maximiser would use the excess profits to take measures, such as advertising, conducive to increasing his sales.

Hall's findings were negative: there was no strong relationship between sales volume and any observed positive departures from the profit constraint. Hall's study, although not lending support to the sales maximisation hypothesis, must not be interpreted as indirect support for the traditional theory of profit maximisation. That the excess profits did not lead to increased sales could be explained, for example, by ineffective advertising (if the excess profits were used for that purpose) or, equally plausibly, that they were used up as perks.

Although the question of how firms respond to a profits tax has been of considerable interest to economic theoreticians,[1] there have been no statistical studies to back up the various assertions made. The traditional theory of the firm based on profit maximising behaviour and its dynamic extension, growth theory of the firm, predict that the introduction of profits tax will not lead to any adjustment in price and output. The models of output, sales and utility maximising behaviour, on the other hand, rule that firms would adjust price and output in the face of such a change. However, the argument which is generally put forward, that businesses would tend to shift this type of tax onto purchasers, is not proof of it actually occurring. More sophisticated testing is needed.

There are two further studies which must be mentioned. The first concerns an attempt by Williamson to lend more than 'casual empiricist' support to his utility maximisation hypothesis.

[12]M. Hall, Sales revenue maximisation: an empirical examination, *Journal of Industrial Economics,* April 1967.
[13]The question of the effects of corporate income tax led to an exchange between F. Sebold and R. Gordon which is contained in the *National Tax Journal,* December 1970.

Williamson, using data for the two largest firms in twenty-six US industries, sought evidence on the extent to which the income of top executives was influenced by the following three factors: concentration ratio in the industry, representation of management on the firms' boards of directors, and the firms' general administrative and selling expenses. All three factors were found to have a positive influence on the remuneration of top executives. The findings might be interpreted as an indication that management responds to opportunities for 'discretionary' behaviour, in this case by increasing the expenditure on highly trained and useful staff. But one ought to bear in mind that the relationship established is, in the first instance, merely a statistical one; no immediate inference about a causal relationship can be made. And of course, while Williamson's interpretation of the findings sounds plausible, there would appear to be an equally convincing interpretation as one of his critics has pointed out:[14]

(i) the relationship between the degree of concentration (or monopoly power) and executive income might be due to the fact that highly skilled executives are needed either to establish or maintain a powerful position and that, to attract or keep the right executives, adequate pay would have to be offered to them;
(ii) the fact that top executives are members of the important decision-making bodies of business organisations and get high salaries could be explained by saying that it would be nonsensical for big firms not to make use of highly trained executives in this way.

The second study (or group of studies) attempts to substantiate the growth theory of the firm. There is a lot of evidence of a relationship between profitability and the growth rate of firms.[15] However, this evidence merely endorses the kind of relationship one would expect to find over a period of time; it does not support a prediction unique to the growth theory.

[14]M. Silver, Managerial discretion and profit maximising behaviour, *Journal of Industrial Economics,* April 1967.
[15]See, for example, A. Singh and G. Whittington, *Growth, Profitability and Valuation,* Cambridge University Press 1968; H.K. Radice, Control type, profitability and growth in large firms: an empirical study, *Economic Journal,* September 1971.

9.6 Conclusions

The traditional theory of the firm based on profit maximising
behaviour has in the last few decades come under attack from
some economists and social scientists. This has led to the
development of a number of alternative models seeking to explain
observed patterns of business behaviour and to yield predictions.
A number of reasons account for the emergence of rival theories.
First of all, it was recognised that in looking at firms' behaviour all
we can say is that a manager like any other individual can be
expected to maximise the satisfaction he gains from his job. Profit
maximisation reflects a particular psychology; it may appear
plausible, but it is nevertheless a very special assumption to
make.[16] That managers achieve maximum satisfaction by
pursuing output, sales, or growth maximisation or by conforming
to the Williamson type behaviour appears equally plausible. The
trend towards considering alternatives to profit maximising
behaviour is also a sign of economists' increased awareness that
price searchers' markets are the rule rather than the exception, so
that one can on longer argue that firms are driven to profit
maximising behaviour via the competitive struggle.[17] A further
realisation has been that with the managerial revolution and its
concomitant divorce of ownership and management, there is no a
priori reason why managers would necessarily pursue the owners
aim of profit maximisation. The second attack on the profit
maximisation notion has emerged not so much from a criticism of
its being based on unrealistic assumptions, but from a questioning
of the realism of some of its conclusions, notably that profits
taxation would leave prices and output unchanged. We have seen
that by assuming output, sales, or utility maximising behaviour we
would, in fact, predict that a profits tax would enter a firm's
decision-making schedule and would influence price and output.

All the alternatives to the profit maximisation model we have
considered seem, on the surface, to offer improvements in that

[16]For a discussion of this point see T. Scitovsky, A note on profit
maximisation and its implications, *Review of Economic Studies,* July - August
1943.
[17]Indeed it can be shown that even under perfect competition (price taker
markets) utility maximisation is sufficient for survival for firms. See the discussion
by G.W. Ladd, Utility maximisation sufficient for competitive survival, *Journal of
Political Economy,* July–August 1969.

they provide more plausible explanations of why and how decisions may be reached by business managers, and seem to yield more realistic predictions about firms' likely responses to change. But, and this is a point one needs to stress, there is not enough evidence as yet to draw any definite conclusions about the relative merits of any of the alternative theories. Too few empirical studies have been undertaken, and the available evidence does not permit us to discriminate between theories, or even between groups of theories. What is called for is an increased emphasis on statistical testing of a discriminating nature.[18]

Why, the reader may ask, are there so few empirical studies of business behaviour? First of all, data are not always easily available; they are also far from perfect. Second, there are conceptual problems involved in applying statistical tests to the predictions of theories of the firm and, in addition to the ones we mentioned earlier in Section 9.4, there is a further basic problem inherent in most actual research: all the models we use to explain business behaviour are applied at the level of the firm, while the statistical studies that are conducted are usually based on data from industry as a whole.[19] Third, the relative neglect of empirical research in economics in general must be regarded as a result of a somewhat distorted scale of values among professional economists which tends to assess empirical research as of intrinsically less worth than model building.[20]

It remains to be seen whether the challenge of empirical research, particularly with respect to testing theories of the firm, will be taken up by economists. It is unlikely that any form of research could establish an overall claim of superiority by any one theory. In dealing with business behaviour we are, after all, dealing with the psychology of business managers, and this is likely to

[18]The need for more statistics on business behaviour has recently been expressed by the Economics Committee of the Social Science Research Council; also by F.G. Davidson, Pricing behaviour: a plea for more statistics, *Economic Record*, December 1969.

[19]We have seen that if all the firms in a market or industry face the same situation, many of the reactions which we have predicted for a single firm would be obscured by secondary effects acting through the market. For a more detailed discussion of the problems of using industry data see G.A. Hay, The dynamics of firm behaviour under alternative cost structures, *American Economic Review*, April 1972.

[20]See W. Leontieff, Theoretical assumptions and non-observed facts, *American Economic Review*, March 1971.

differ. The search is, therefore, for the 'appropriateness' of a particular model for a given problem, to explain observed behaviour and accurately to predict future behaviour. For some purposes, as we have shown, it is perfectly adequate to assume profit maximisation as the managers' goal: it enables us to construct a rather simple model which nevertheless helps us to explain firms' responses to demand and cost changes and to throw light on the phenomenon of price discrimination, for which there is ample evidence. On the other hand, other features of business behaviour, such as managers' preference for perks, cannot be explained by relying on the profit maximisation model. And the prediction of this model, that profits taxation will not affect price and output decisions, does not seem plausible in practice and is certainly at variance with casual empiricist observations.

But until some evidence is forthcoming, the debate over this question will continue. There is, in short, plenty of scope for useful work relating to the economics of the firm.

Suggestions for further reading
Empirical research in economics

F. Machlup, Marginal analysis and empirical research, *American Economic Review*, March 1946.

F. Machlup, The problem of verification in economics, *Southern Economic Journal*, July 1955.

R.G. Lipsey, *Introduction to Positive Economics* (3rd edn), Weidenfeld and Nicolson 1971.

B. Ward, *What's Wrong with Economics?*, Macmillan 1972.

G.D.N. Worswick, Is progress in economic science possible? *Economic Journal*, March 1972.

Questionnaire studies and interviews

R. Lester, Shortcomings of marginal analysis for wage-employment problems, *American Economic Review*, March 1946.

R.L. Hall and C.J. Hitch, Price theory and business behaviour, *Oxford Economic Papers*, May 1939

R.B. Heflebower, Full costs, cost changes and prices, *Business Concentration and Price Behaviour*, National Bureau of Economic Research 1955.

D.C. Hague, *Pricing in Business*, Allen and Unwin 1971.

A.D.H. Kaplan, J.B. Dirlam and R.F. Lanzillotti, *Pricing in Big Business*, The Brookings Institution 1958.

C.I. Savage and J.R. Small, *Introduction to Managerial Economics*, Hutchinson 1967. (See Chapter 9).

J.S. Earley, Marginal policies of 'excellently managed companies', *American Economic Review*, March 1956.

Statistical studies

O.E. Williamson, *The Economics of Discretionary Behaviour*, Prentice Hall 1964.

M. Silver, Managerial discretion and profit maximising behaviour, *Journal of Industrial Economics*, April 1967.

J.W. McGuire, et al., Executive incomes, sales and profits, *American Economic Review*, September 1962.

E.S. Mills, *Price, Output and Inventory Policy: A Study of the Economics of the Firm and Industry*, Wiley 1962.

P.J. Lund and F. Rushdy, The effect of demand on prices in British manufacturing industry, *Review of Economic Studies*, October 1967.

B.D. Mabry and D.L. Siders, An empirical test of the SM hypothesis, *Southern Economic Journal*, January 1967.

M. Hall, Sales revenue maximisation: an empirical examination, *Journal of Industrial Economics*, April 1967.

L. Wavermann, Sales revenue maximisation: a note, *Journal of Industrial Economics*, November 1968.

L. Phlips, Business pricing policies and inflation: some evidence from EEC countries, *Journal of Industrial Economics*, November 1969.

Advanced theory of the firm

R.M. Cyert and C.I. Hendrick, Theory of the firm: past, present and future: an interpretation, *Journal of Economic Literature*, June 1972.

R.M. Solow, Some implications of alternative criteria for the firm, in R.L. Marris and A. Wood (eds), *The Corporate Economy: Growth, Competition and Innovative Potential*, Harvard University Press 1971.

R.L. Marris, Why economics needs a theory of the firm, *Economic Journal*, March 1972.

H.A. Simon, Theories of decision making in economics and behavioural science, *American Economic Review*, June 1959.

E. Furubotn and S. Pejovich, Property rights and economic theory: a survey of recent literature, *Journal of Economic Literature*, December 1972.

A. Silberston, Price behaviour of firms, *Economic Journal*, September 1970.

J.R. Wildsmith, *Managerial Theories of the Firm*, Martin Robertson 1973.

K.J. Cohen and R.M. Cyert, *Theory of the Firm*, Prentice Hall 1965.

R.M. Cyert and J.G. March, *A Behavioural Theory of the Firm*, Prentice Hall 1963.

M. Shubik, Objective functions and models of corporate organisations, *Quarterly Journal of Economics*, August 1961.

J.W. McGuire (ed), *Interdisciplinary Studies in Business Behaviour*, South Western Publishing Company 1962.

W.L. Baldwin, The motives of managers, environmental constraints and the theory of managerial enterprise, *Quarterly Journal of Economics*, May 1964.

F. Machlup, Theories of the firm: marginalist, behavioural, managerial, *American Economic Review*, March 1967.

G.C. Archibald (ed.), *Theory of the Firm*, Penguin 1971

Index